j540
C

Corrick, James A.

Recent revolutions
in chemistry

87-0925

DATE			

RECENT REVOLUTIONS
IN CHEMISTRY

RECENT REVOLUTIONS IN CHEMISTRY
James A. Corrick

FRANKLIN WATTS 1986
NEW YORK   LONDON
TORONTO   SYDNEY
A SCIENCE IMPACT BOOK

Photographs courtesy of:
Michigan Division of Dow Chemical U.S.A.: pp. 10, 32;
California Institute of Technology: p. 20; Extrel Corporation: p. 22; Computer Graphics Laboratory, University
of California, San Francisco, © Regents, University of
California: p. 24; Union Carbide Corporation: p. 30;
NASA: pp. 33, 48, 49, 95; San Francisco Opera Company:
p. 36; Mark S. Wrighton, MIT: p. 40; Instron Corporation:
p. 45; U.S. Army: pp. 51, 52; Oak Ridge National Labo-
ratory: pp. 58, 106; Brookhaven National Laboratory: pp.
61, 62, 67; National Oceanographic and Atmospheric
Administration: p. 72; The Bettmann Archive: pp. 76, 79;
Dow Corning Corporation, Midland, Michigan: p. 84;
IBM: p. 87; The University of Illinois; p. 98; USDA-Soil
Conservation Service: p. 99; Steve Delaney/EPA: p. 104;
Department of Energy: pp. 112, 113; University of California, Lawrence Berkeley Laboratory: p. 115.

Library of Congress Cataloging in Publication Data

Corrick, James.
Recent revolutions in chemistry.

(A Science impact book)
Bibliography: p.
Includes index.
Summary: Describes the different branches of chemistry
and discusses recent theories and discoveries and their
practical uses.
1. Chemistry—Juvenile literature. [1. Chemistry]
I. Title. II Series.
QD35.C68 1986   540   86-5675
ISBN 0-531-10241-6

CONTENTS

87-0925

CHAPTER 1
OUR CHEMICAL WORLD

*I*t could be any day—even today—and any place. At a race-track, a driver steps on the accelerator, and the car leaps into the lead with a roar from its plastic engine. At a drugstore downtown, a woman buys a new brand of tissues that will keep her from spreading her cold to her family. In another part of the state, two researchers sit in their university laboratory and run tests to find out the age of cloth fragments found recently on a dig in the Middle East. In the Arctic, Air Force technicians line a temporary runway with self-contained, nuclear-powered landing lights. And in orbit, an astronaut checks the progress of crystals growing in a large test tube.

Although none of these activities are related, they do have something in common, and that thing is chemistry. Every one of the products and processes mentioned above comes from the study and understanding of chemistry. The plastic engine and the cold-inhibiting tissues, both of which are being field tested right now, come from an understanding of chemical structure. Nuclear chemistry produced the Air Force's new landing lights, and analytical chemistry created the techniques used in dating archaeological finds. The astronaut is performing a chemical experiment in growing crystals.

CHEMISTRY

We all have a vague idea of what chemistry is. In a general way, we think of it as men and women in white lab coats

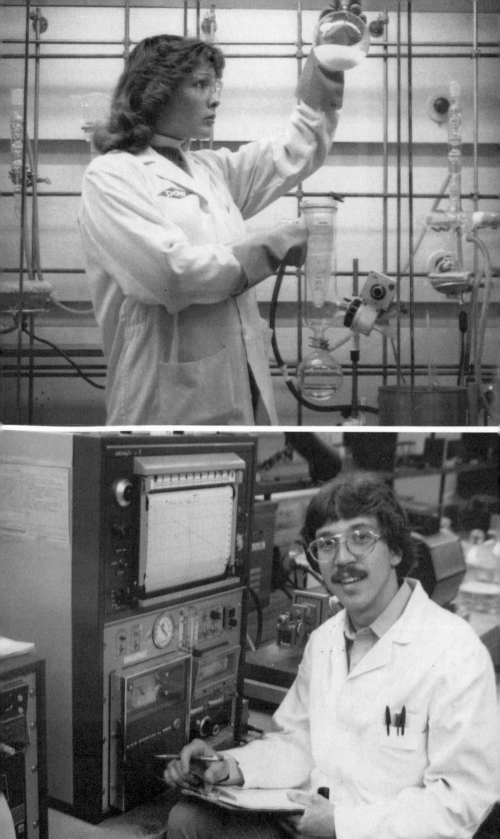

playing with test tubes and beakers full of strange, fuming liquids. We think of rooms full of complicated arrangements of glass tubing, out of which a few drops of some potent chemical finally emerge.

For the most part, however, these pictures are pure Hollywood. They present a distorted view of modern chemistry filtered through bad science fiction and horror movies. The reality, although it may appear less dramatic, is actually far more interesting and certainly more important to each and every one of us. What *is* chemistry?

Chemistry is the science that gives us a picture of the composition of various substances. It is the study of the structure and properties of all the materials that make up our world. Through chemistry, we know that water is a combination of hydrogen and oxygen; that gasoline consists of carbon, hydrogen, and oxygen; that common table salt is made from sodium and chlorine.

But chemistry tells us more than just the makeup of those things that surround us. It lets us know how substances interact to form other materials. Thus, from chemistry, we know that a burning piece of wood is the rapid combination of oxygen in the air with the carbon and hydrogen making up that wood and that this burning produces both water and carbon dioxide. Ultimately, then, chemistry lets us understand our world better.

THE CHEMICAL CENTURY

As essential as such understanding is, it is not the only importance of chemistry. Without chemistry, our modern

Although chemistry is a complex science and there are all kinds of chemists, some chemists still wear the proverbial white lab coat and work with complicated equipment and beakers full of liquids. Both people pictured here work for the Dow Chemical company.

twentieth-century world would be very different indeed. The products of applied chemistry surround us. Not one of us can get through a day without using dozens of such products.

Looks like rain? Put that folded, lightweight, plastic raincoat with your books. Have a headache? Take an aspirin. Have an ant problem? Spray them with that can of insecticide. Trying to watch your weight? Drink that diet cola with the nonsugar sweetener.

All of these and more come from the processing vats of the chemical industry.

Our world of the 1980s is radically different from the world of 1900. In part, this difference is itself a chemical product. We have a diversity of materials and processes created through chemical research and development that were completely unknown at the beginning of the century.

At present, chemists have identified some 5 million chemical substances, most discovered within the last 75 years. Of that 5 million, however, only 5,000 have commercial applications. Still, with this one-tenth of one percent, we have made things that couldn't exist in 1900 because the naturally occurring materials of that period do not have the strength or lightness to match our present-day chemical synthetics.

Because of chemistry, we have jetliners, space shuttles, and artificial earth satellites, as well as more commonplace items such as mini stereo/cassette players. Such players exist only because of solid-state electronics, based on the silicon chip, and lightweight materials for earphones—chemical products all.

THE SUBMERGED SCIENCE

If chemistry has become the foundation upon which we have erected our modern world, it has also become more and more entangled with other sciences and disciplines. As we shall see, it is almost impossible to speak of a pure science called chemistry. Not that there is any lack of chemical research, but much of it is involved with everything from geology to archaeology to art. We have electronic engineers using chemistry to create more and more sophisticated integrated circuits; biological scientists turning to chemistry to understand living organisms; anthropologists discovering through chemistry what game our ancestors hunted.

Chemistry has become a part of many other sciences and disciplines. Nor is this surprising. To study and understand the physical nature of any object, whether living or not, ultimately requires chemistry, since all things are composed of chemicals.

Often when we speak of revolutions in chemistry, we are talking about revolutions in other fields. When in the early 1950s, James Watson and Francis Crick determined the chemical structure of *DNA*, the material that passes on inherited characteristics in plants and animals, they had taken not just an important step in the study of chemistry but also in biology. With the structure of DNA known, biologists were able to learn more about biological inheritance than at any time in the past. Both chemists and biologists were finally on the path that has led to their actually working with DNA in genetic engineering.

This is not to say that chemistry has disappeared. Rather, as with so many other twentieth-century fields, it has fragmented into areas of specialization. In one sense, we cannot talk about a single science called chemistry. Instead, it is made up of a great number of "chemistries." We have, for example, one devoted to the chemistry of living things, another to the mechanics of chemical reactions, still another to the properties of substances containing carbon.

This fragmentation or specialization is one of the important revolutions in chemistry. It has led to the intense study of certain areas of chemistry that in themselves have become important revolutions in the science. Thus, the study of carbon-containing substances has led to revolutions in both plastics and drug manufacturing. Nuclear chemistry has, for better or worse, revolutionized the world. The study of the chemistry of silicon has given us in the last two decades an electronics revolution.

As we go through this book, we will look not only at these major chemical revolutions, but also at a number of smaller changes wrought by chemistry. And we will see that few things concern us that are also not affected by these chemical revolutions.

If chemistry has changed into a collection of specialties, what about chemists? Not surprisingly, they too have become specialists. In the nineteenth century and even during the first few decades of this century, one could speak of chemists as scientists who knew all there was to know about this one particular science. But no one man or woman has either the time or the ability to learn all there is to know about all of the subjects that now lie under the banner of chemistry. It is doubtful if any one person could fully master even one of the major specialty areas—there is too much information.

Modern chemists are often more than just knowledgeable about chemistry; they may know as much about biology or physics or geology as about chemistry. Some, such as Francis Crick, who was originally a physicist, do not even begin in chemistry, but come to it because it offers them answers to their research problems.

These modern chemists spend much less time than did their predecessors working directly with chemicals, testing properties and structure. Instead, as we shall see in chapter 2, they depend on machines and computers to do such work since these instruments are more reliable and accurate than the older "chemical" methods.

Whether it is the lone chemist working in a small university laboratory or a large team of scientists and technicians working for industry or the government and whatever the methods used, we should always remember that the revolutions of chemistry are a human product. There is always a human being or beings behind each and every advance in chemistry. So, let us see what these chemists have been creating in their labs these past few years.

CHAPTER 2
UNLOCKING
THE
MOLECULE

Bright primary colors—red, green, blue—tint the geometrical pattern. Looking almost like a stained-glass window from some medieval cathedral, it floats in the monitor screen while the two chemists study it.

"There," says one, using a pointer to indicate a small red and green area.

"Right." The other fingers a button, and the pattern on the screen twists and rotates until now it looks like a string of fat grapes fused together.

"That's it," says the first chemist. "If we can get rid of that branch of atoms, we'll have our drug."

As the two continue watching the computer-simulated chemical model, they begin discussing how they can chemically manufacture their new drug.

Until now, scenes such as this have appeared only in science fiction movies such as *The Andromeda Strain* and *Outland*, and although computer-assisted chemical designing is still some years off, computer graphics are beginning to open up chemical structure for visual examination.

Indeed, computer simulation is only the most recent step in one of the major chemical revolutions of the twentieth century—the unlocking of the prime chemical building block, the *molecule*. It is the chemist's increasing understanding and continuing study of how molecules are constructed and how they interact that has made ours the chemical century. Without such knowledge, chemists could only discover and produce new chemicals through trial-and-error experimentation, and thus, until this century, chemistry was almost entirely a science of accidental discovery.

THE ATOM

The first key to unlocking the molecule was the determination of the structure of the *atom*. Coming from the Greek word *atomos*, meaning "that which cannot be divided," the atom is the smallest particle of matter that can undergo a chemical reaction.

Of course, we now know that each atom is made of a great many subatomic particles, but the chemist is only interested in the three primary particles, the *electron*, the *proton*, and the *neutron*.

Both the electron and the proton have electrical charges, the electron being negatively charged and the proton positively charged. The neutron has no charge. Since an atom, like a neutron, is neutral, it has an equal number of protons and electrons. Thus, the negative and positive charges cancel each other out.

Two British scientists, Lord Rutherford and Sir James Chadwick, showed in the early decades of this century that the protons and neutrons cluster together at the atom's center. This center is the *atomic nucleus* (plural, nuclei).

Other research revealed that, the larger the atom, the greater the number of protons and neutrons in that atomic nucleus. Each atom has a specific number of protons, known as its *atomic number*. For example, each atom of hydrogen has 1 proton, each atom of helium 2, carbon 6, and uranium, the largest naturally occurring atom, 92.

Atomic numbers are extremely important to the chemist because they distinguish between *chemical elements*. By definition an element is made up of atoms all having the same atomic number. Such substances are at the end of the chemical line since no amount of effort can break them down by chemical means.

And where are the electrons? Orbiting that very same nucleus (see Figure 1).

No electron, however, has an exact orbital path such as a planet like the earth has around the sun. Rather, each one moves through a volume of space around the nucleus. Each atomic nucleus is surrounded by a cloud of electrons, not unlike a beehive encircled by swarming bees.

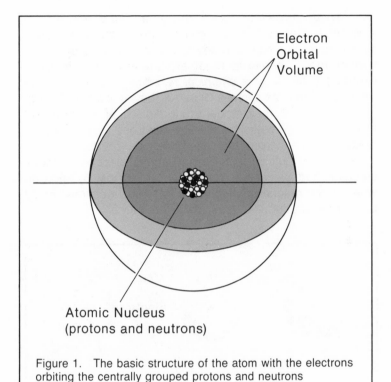

Figure 1. The basic structure of the atom with the electrons orbiting the centrally grouped protons and neutrons

COMBINATIONS

And molecules?

You rarely find individual atoms in nature. Instead, they are normally linked to other atoms, and such groups of linked atoms are molecules. Any substance composed entirely of one type of molecule is called a *chemical compound*.

Two hydrogen atoms link with one oxygen atom to form a molecule of water, and any body of water contains millions, if not billions, of these hydrogen-oxygen molecules. Likewise, the gas we exhale while breathing, carbon dioxide, is a compound made up of molecules that all have one carbon atom linked to two oxygen atoms.

How do molecules form? Because of the work of the nineteenth-century British chemist John Dalton, early twentieth-century chemists already knew that when they mixed two or more chemicals together, the molecules involved exchanged atoms in a *chemical reaction*. But not until the 1920s did chemists such as Gilbert N. Lewis and Irving Langmuir, armed with their model of atomic structure, show that atoms form molecules by sharing electrons (see Figure 2). Such shared electrons are called *chemical bonds*.

Chemists quickly learned how many electrons various elements had available to form chemical bonds. By knowing what atoms reacting molecules contained, a chemist could predict the product—at least part of the time.

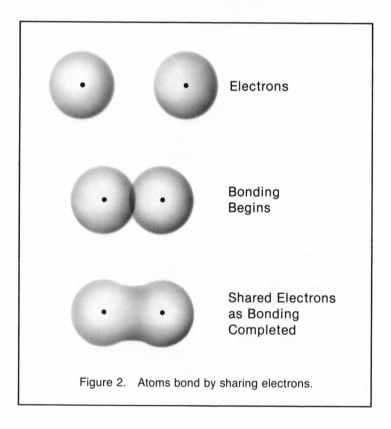

Electrons

Bonding
Begins

Shared Electrons
as Bonding
Completed

Figure 2.   Atoms bond by sharing electrons.

Unfortunately, as Linus Pauling pointed out in 1939 in his landmark book *The Nature of the Chemical Bond*, bonding is complicated by the three-dimensional structure of molecules. Reacting molecules are not unlike a key and a lock. A particular key is cut to fit the tumblers of a particular lock—your front door key does not fit your neighbor's front door lock and vice versa. So it is with molecules. If the molecule key is not "cut" right—does not have the right three-dimensional structure—it will not fit into the molecule lock.

Pauling's findings mean that, for a chemist to design a reaction to produce a desired chemical compound, that chemist must know the types and arrangement of atoms in the molecules with which he or she is working. And chemistry has been increasingly successful in discovering these matters, particularly since the end of World War II.

BREAKING IN

Looking inside the molecule is no easy trick since even the largest, containing a million-plus atoms, are barely visible under the most powerful modern microscope. Most are completely invisible even under high magnification. Therefore, the chemist needs special equipment.

The modern chemical laboratory is dominated by such sophisticated instruments, which allow the chemist to find out what elements make up any particular compound, what chemical bonds are involved, and what atomic arrangements exist. Most of the major chemical instruments—the mass spectrometer, the X-ray spectrometer, and the nuclear magnetic resonance spectrometer—have been in use for at least twenty years, but recent innovations have increased both their accuracy and speed.

The *mass spectrometer* works by literally splitting a molecule into fragments and then identifying the atomic makeup of these fragments. A chemist needing to know the molecular composition of, say, a recently discovered antibiotic would pop a sample into the mass spectrometer and, after a few minutes' wait, would have a readout with that information.

However, chemical compounds rarely come in neat little

Dr. Linus Pauling, whose investigations into the nature of the chemical bond paved the way for the creation of many of the chemicals and other products that are so much a part of our modern world. Pauling, shown here with the kind of molecular model always associated with him, won the Nobel Prize in chemistry in 1954.

packages. Rather, they are found naturally in a mix with other compounds. The chemist then must first separate the desired compound from those others.

Until the early 1980s, chemical researchers would pour this mix into a *gas chromatography column*. Molecules of different sizes pass down such a column at different speeds, and thus each compound in a chemical mixture leaves the column at different times. The chemist would wait for the above antibiotic to come off the chromatography column and then put it into the mass spectrometer.

Now, however, a new, faster method of separation and analysis has come to the chemistry lab. Two mass spectrometers are linked together, with the first separating out the right compound and the second doing the actual analysis.

The *tandem mass spectrometer*, as it is called, has advantages over the older mass spectrometer–gas chromatography combination. First, it can work with as few as three molecules mixed in with ten trillion others. Such precision is particularly useful in discovering the amount of chemical pollutants in contaminated soil, since the toxic level of such wastes as dioxin is only one molecule in a trillion.

Second, the tandem mass spectrometer provides faster analysis than the older system. Gas chromatography columns take several minutes to several hours to work. The tandem instrument separates mixtures almost instantaneously. Since most chemists prefer to run several samples of a compound through analysis to check and recheck their results, such speed means the total time consumed by several runs will only be an hour or two rather than most of a day. Also, in cases where a large number of samples must be run—as in pollutant monitoring—less time for analysis is required, so decisions may be made more quickly.

AND THE X-RAY
SHOWS . . .

As useful as the mass spectrometer is, it does not work with very large molecules such as *proteins*. Since proteins are one of the major classes of chemicals found in animals and plants and are important in the manufacture of many drugs

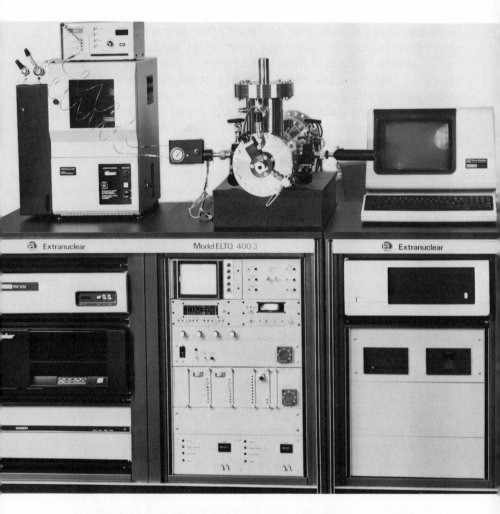

A mass spectrometer system. On the counter, from left to right, are the chromatograph, mass spectrometer, and computer terminal. Beneath the spectrometer itself are its controls. The data system is on either side of the spectrometer controls. The little monitor in the upper-left-hand corner of the spectrometer control unit allows you to see the spectra as they are generated.

such as insulin, chemists need to learn as much as they can about them. Such knowledge is difficult to obtain about these molecules, many of which have hundreds of thousands, sometimes up to a million, atoms within them.

The *X-ray spectrometer* has proven valuable in studying these large molecules. The X-rays pass through the sample under study and form an image on a photographic plate of film. The results show the location of clusters of electrons, which indicate the location of not only the atoms in the molecule, but the chemical bonds as well.

At Lawrence Livermore National Laboratory, a team of scientists headed by Dennis L. Matthews is seeking to improve the X-ray spectrometer by using an X-ray laser. With the addition of Matthews' laser, this particular instrument is not only becoming more precise, but it will soon be producing holograms—laser-generated, three-dimensional pictures—of the inside of molecules. The detail promises to be impressive.

MAKE IT GRAPHIC

Wendy L. Freedman and Barry F. Madore are astronomers at the University of Toronto, and their only goal in 1982 was to write a computer program that would trace the evolution of a spiral galaxy like our own. They succeeded. Soon, however, they discovered that their program could also provide far more. It could also supply computer graphic displays of the progress of certain chemical reactions that form spiral patterns.

As with most sciences, chemistry has benefited from the computer, particularly in the last decade with the development of smaller and smaller computers with larger and larger memories. Such machines as the Perkins-Elmer Corporation's Series 7000 with its Pecuv program have been the single most important improvement in chemical analysis of molecules.

Computer-assisted instruments are both fast and reliable. They can make as many as 100,000 measurements in a short period of time. No human chemist could approach this number, no matter how many years he or she had.

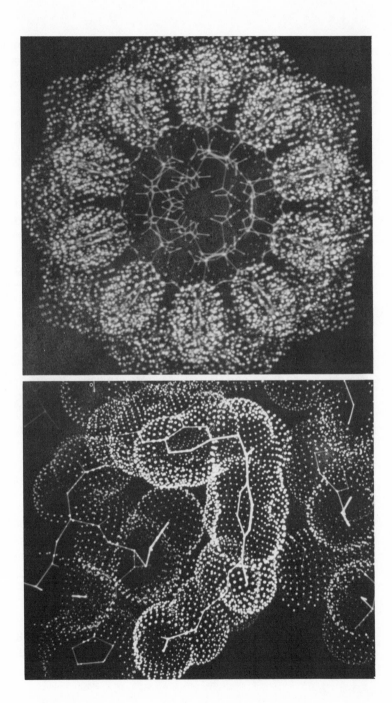

The computer also has allowed chemists to look at the atomic arrangements in molecules.

As early as 1964, Cyrus Levinthal of MIT was having his computer generate three-dimensional graphic representations of complex molecules. Now, almost twenty years later, a hundred centers exist to provide computer-generated graphics of molecules.

Where Levinthal's images were composed of all blacks and whites, making it difficult to figure out what atoms were bonded to what other atoms, the current graphics are color coded. Oxygen is red, carbon is green, and nitrogen is blue.

The computer can also be instructed to move around and through the molecular images. You can see a molecule from the top, the bottom, the side. You can float through the center. You can look at specific sections.

All of this has led to a better understanding of molecular structure and of the ways that molecules react. Elizabeth Getzoff of the Research Institute of Scripps Clinic believes that such a computer-generated graphic "told her" how a specific protein—a possible cancer fighter—operates. The simulation revealed an unsuspected valley into which another molecule could fit like a key into a lock.

Aided by increasingly sophisticated computer-assisted instrumentation, the twentieth-century chemist continues looking into molecule after molecule. Through such a search, chemists are building up a more and more complete picture of how chemical compounds are constructed and how they come to act as they do. With such knowledge comes more and more control over the design of chemical compounds to fit the needs of our world.

Computer-generated images of molecules.
The originals are in color, with each
color representing either a type of atom
or the location of a particular process.

CHAPTER 3
FORGING CHEMICAL CHAINS

THE MOLECULE MECHANICS

Eyes narrowed against the glare, the village smith intently watches the bar of iron resting on the bed of glowing coals. Dark and cold a few minutes ago, the bar is now almost white-hot.

"Faster!" the smith orders a gasping, sweat-slicked apprentice pumping the forge's bellows.

In the heat-distorted air, the iron bar seems to waver and jump frantically about. Finally, it is white-hot, and with long tongs, the smith reaches in and pulls out the bar. The smith places it on an iron anvil and, with steady downward swings, begins to hammer it into shape.

So it was at one time: the village smith in the forge, turning cold iron into everything from nails and barrel rungs to sword blades and rifle muzzles. Now it is the chemist, using his or her knowledge of molecular structure, who builds the products of our modern world.

Need a hard, transparent, shatterproof lens for eyeglasses? A soft, durable, wash-and-wear shirt? An all-weather lubricating oil? Turn to twentieth-century chemistry and its molecular engineers. These products and many more would not exist today except for the chemist's ability to manipulate that chemical building block—the molecule.

And nowhere has this manufacturing revolution been more active than in the creation of *plastic* and plastic goods.

THE CHAIN THAT BINDS

Plastic, once a novelty of the 1939 New York World's Fair, is now so commonplace that we humorously describe the last half of the twentieth century as the Plastic Age. Plastics are actually one class of a chemical group called *polymers.* The prefix *poly* means "many," and these compounds contain many carbon atoms bonded together in long chains (see Figure 3). Plastics are not the only polymers; proteins, natural rubber, and DNA are all examples of polymers.

The actual number of carbon atoms forming the spine of individual polymers varies, but 50,000 is a good working average. A chain implies that polymers are long, straight molecules, and indeed, some of them are. But molecular structure is more complicated than this, and polymers have three basic structures (see Figure 4).

The linear polymer does exist. It is not a straight chain, but a looping thread not unlike a wadded-up piece of string. The branched polymer has short chains—branches—projecting off of the main chain; these polymers are generally stronger than the linear since these branches act as cross-bracing.

The final polymer type, the network, looks much like a road map. Such polymers are very flexible, and their structure is the basis of the give-and-take properties of rubber. When pressure is applied to rubber, its myriad of crosslinks

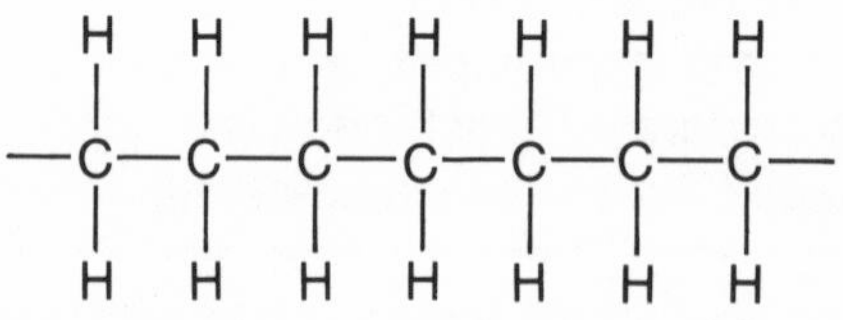

Figure 3.   Polymers are long chains of carbon atoms (C) bonded one to another. Such chains run on the average 50,000 carbon atoms. Hydrogen (H) is also a common element in polymers.

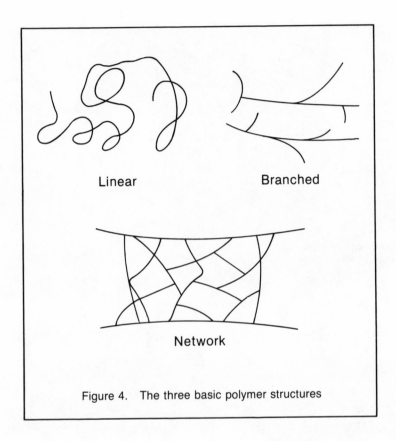

Linear

Branched

Network

Figure 4. The three basic polymer structures

slide, and when released, they pull back into place. Rubber can be compressed or rolled or squashed, but it still snaps back into its original shape.

What sets a plastic apart from other polymers is its ability to be molded under pressure or heat into various shapes from buttons to knobs to car bodies. Modern plastics, unlike earlier plastics, are durable because they do not decompose in air, water, or sunlight.

Unfortunately, this very durability has created its own problem. Discarded plastic bottles, containers, and even auto parts pose a disposal problem. Albert Spaak of the Plastics Institute of America is hoping that ways may soon be

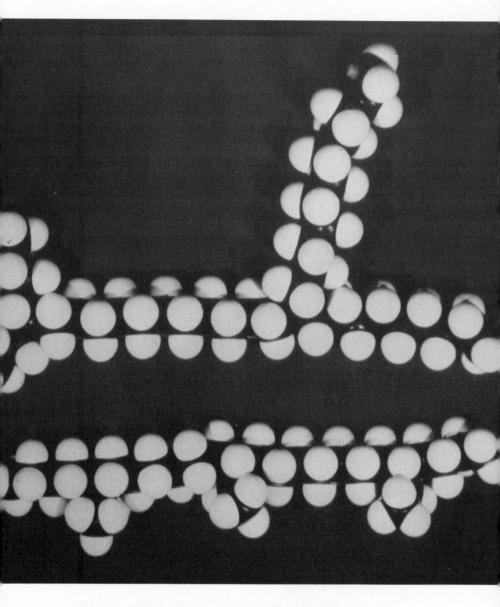

Models of two types of polyethylene. The type shown on the bottom has a structure that makes for a rubbery, low-density material.

found to recycle such plastic. This plastic trash when remelted and remolded is not as durable as the original plastic, but Spaak and the Plastics Institute are testing the possibility of using this secondhand plastic to fill pillows, insulate sleeping bags and coats, and make window shutters.

As we shall see in the next chapter, the new plastics' durability and strength are making them one of the most important structural materials in the 1980s. In many instances, plastics are replacing metals because they can take more physical abuse—without permanent damage—than many older building materials.

But plastics have more uses than providing walls for buildings and interior panels on airplanes.

A LITTLE LESS GRAVITY, PLEASE

In April 1983, when the space shuttle *Challenger* landed, there were billions of microscopic things aboard. No, the spacecraft was not infested with some pest; rather, it brought back the first commercial product made in orbit: incredibly tiny plastic spheres, each measuring 10 microns in diameter (1/2,500 of an inch).

The spheres were part of an experiment designed by John W. Vanderhoff of Lehigh University. Each sphere began as a small seed of polystyrene—the same plastic used to make polystyrene foam packing for shipping fragile items—to which more polystyrene was added after the *Challenger* reached orbit. The spheres were then heated for twenty hours.

The result was perfect spheres that were supplied to the National Bureau of Standards to sell (a vial of 3,000,000 spheres went for $350 in 1985). Since the dimension of each sphere is known perfectly, they will act as tiny tape measures to check the precision of delicate instruments used in determining the size of human blood cells, as well as microscopic particles of silver in photographic film, pigments in paint, and pollutants from the air.

Why make these spheres in space?

Oddly enough, despite their minuteness, they are too

Left: *Polyethylene is being blown by air to form a column. One familiar product that might be manufactured using such a process is garbage bags.*
Right: *Threads of polycarbonate (a type of plastic) being cooled before being turned into pellets and sold as CALIBRE, a Dow Chemical product*

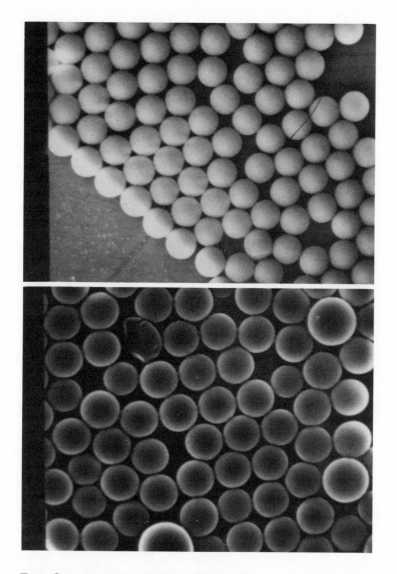

Top: *Space-produced latex particles are identical, "perfect."* Bottom: *Latex particles made on Earth with the same equipment and process show the influence of gravity: they are deformed or off-sized or show other imperfections.*

large to be made on the earth. Plastic spheres greater than 3 microns in diameter either distort under the earth's gravity, becoming egg-shaped, or clump together. Under zero-g (zero gravitational force), not only are the 10-micron spheres possible, but so are ones up to 100 microns, which are equally impossible to manufacture here.

FOAMING ACTION

Polystyrene has proven useful for other purposes than calibrating measuring instruments. In its foam form, it has been effective in raising sunken ships.

Some years ago, a freighter carrying sheep sank in Kuwait harbor. Traditionally, sunken ships are raised by pumping them full of air. Such a procedure requires the total sealing of the ship to prevent the air from leaking out and leaving the ship on the bottom. All in all, an expensive process.

Enter polystyrene foam.

The foaming action that creates this plastic is due to bubbles of air being caught and suspended in the polymer. These air bubbles are trapped in the polystyrene foam and form hundreds of little pockets. Because of this trapped air, this foam floats in water.

Instead of air, then, the sunken ship in Kuwait harbor was pumped full of polystyrene beads. The foam's trapped air provided the necessary buoyancy to raise the ship to the surface without the need for extensive sealing of the craft. Other salvage operations have been equally successful using this technique.

SUPPORTING THE ARTS

Joan Clark did not want to raise a sunken ship or calibrate an instrument. As an occupational therapist, she wanted lightweight splints and supports for broken fingers and sprained joints and she wanted something that could be molded easily and quickly in place.

Her husband, John Clark, president of Polygon Manufacturing Company, a plastics plant, gave her Polyform. At room temperature, this plastic is strong and rigid, but at 160° Fahrenheit (F) (71° Celsius, or C), it becomes soft. A doctor can mold a Polyform splint around a broken finger or form a support for a twisted knee from this chemical mix of plastic and rubber (the actual formula is a trade secret).

Polyform, along with a second product, Hexcelete, has succeeded in largely replacing the old, cumbersome, and heavy plaster cast for many injuries—a small revolution, but a comforting one to those in need of such splints and supports.

These two developments of the late 1970s have found a new use in the 1980s.

Tom Collins, who designs and constructs the sets, props, and costuming for the San Francisco Opera, realized that both Polyform and Hexcelete could be molded into everything from authentic-looking armor for the actors to swords and spears to fake columns. Where in the past, Collins and his staff took hours to make such stage accessories, now they did the same job in minutes. Armor breastplates and helmets are molded directly to the actor's body and head and are thereafter a perfect fit.

Other theaters, as well as drama departments producing school plays, have followed Collins's lead. Not only are these plastic costumes and props lightweight, they are easily repaired simply by reheating and remolding. Also, because of the ease of working with these plastics, plays can now enjoy an elaborate realism confined previously to the most expensively produced movies. What was and is a source of practical benefit to many people is now contributing to the entertainment of even more.

HIGH-CALIBER
PROTECTION

In 1977, police officer David Schafer was not thinking about theater costuming. Rather, he was thankful he had been wearing a vest woven from a synthetic polymer, Kevlar. A suspect had shot Schafer with a .45-caliber automatic from only 6 inches (15 centimeters) away. The shot was true, but it left the police officer with only a bruise and a small burn.

Donkey's head made by Tom Collins for the
San Francisco Opera. The head is made of
a plastic called Vara-Form, which eliminates
the need for a substructure.

Since its discovery by Stephanie Kwalek, Kevlar has become the most important fabric for making bulletproof vests. Such vests are as light as nylon, but are five times stronger than steel. They are able to stop almost any bullet except those from high-powered rifles.

In 1982, the U.S. Army scrapped its old steel helmets that had been in use since World War II and replaced them with Kevlar-plastic helmets, which first saw successful use in combat in the 1983 invasion of Grenada.

Kevlar does have less ominous applications. It is replacing steel cords in belted-radial tires, as well as being turned into sails and hockey sticks.

SOMETHING TO WEAR

When we think of synthetic fibers such as nylon or polyester, we normally think about clothing. Yet, although nylon goes into making pantyhose and parachutes, it also finds its way into our lives as plastic machine parts—many bicycles now have nylon chain sprockets that are stronger and more durable than those made from steel. Polyester is the basis not only for wash-and-wear clothing, but also for magnetic recording tape.

Nylon, polyester, and other synthetic fibers are polymers like any other plastic and, when not manufactured as threads, are used to make plastic products. Traditional plastics such as polyethylene (used to make food storage bags, among many other things) make excellent protective industrial clothing.

When most people think of protective clothing, they want clothes to keep them warm or cool. Tyrone L. Vigo of the U.S. Department of Agriculture is presently developing a new plastic fabric that will protect the wearer from both arctic cold and steel mill heat, and will do it four times better than any present protective clothing.

Vigo has woven his fabric from rayon threads filled with plastic. When this plastic core is exposed to high temperatures, it uses this heat to chemically change its form; thus, none of the heat escapes through the fabric to the wearer. In low temperatures, the plastic returns to its original chemical form, and in doing so, it releases heat, thus warming the wearer.

Vigo's first use of this new fabric, however, will not be as hot and cold weather clothing. He intends to make animal and plant shelters. Farmers will be able to erect these shelters easily and quickly to protect their herds and crops from unexpected rises and drops in temperature.

A FINE COAT

In the 1980s, we dress not only our bodies with synthetic polymers, but also our houses. The latex paints we see advertised on TV and in magazines are suspensions of one or more polymers such as polystyrene in water. The polymer by itself is too thick to spread well and must be diluted with water to make an effective paint.

These water-based paints have many advantages over older paints. Unlike oil paints, latex paints are more durable, dry faster, and do not require messy, often smelly chemicals for cleanup. Unlike lead paints, these new paints are not poisonous—more than one child has died from eating lead-based paints. Latex paints also do not leave a persistent odor and are not flammable.

Modern chemists, however, have not stopped with latex paints. They have gone on to design paints for special purposes. Do you need a paint that does not scorch under high temperatures? The chemist has a paint that will resist the heat of ovens, heaters, and engines. Do you need a fire-retardant paint? Again, the chemist has developed such paints. One kind, upon catching fire, releases gases that smother the fire. Another fuses into a glasslike surface, cutting off the fire from its fuel.

THE PLASTIC CURRENT

Over the years, chemists have discovered that plastics offer some surprising possibilities. One of these is the conduction of electricity.

Anyone who looks at modern electrical wiring can see that it is insulated by a plastic covering. Plastics make good insulators because, unlike metals, they hold tightly to their electrons. By definition, electricity is the free flow of electrons, so any substance that does not permit such an electron flow cannot be an electrical conductor.

However, chemists wondered if polymers could not be chemically treated so as to loosen their electron grip. In 1964, John Lupinski and Kenneth Kopple did make a polymer that conducted electricity.

A number of such plastic conductors have come out of chemistry labs since then. Until recently, they have remained chemical curiosities because they tend to break up in air and water. To make them is also both expensive and difficult.

Within the last two years, however, Alan G. MacDiarmid of the University of Pennsylvania has created a conducting polymer suffering from none of these problems. MacDiarmid's plastic is even ten times more efficient than previous attempts.

The ease with which this polymer is made may mean that this Pennsylvania chemist is on the road to discovering an inexpensive method for making rechargeable batteries. Presently, rechargeable batteries cost two to three times more than the throwaway kind. Already MacDiarmid has made a rechargeable flashlight that, according to him, works very well.

MacDiarmid is not the only chemist having success with conducting polymers. Mark S. Wrighton and his MIT team have built a transistor that uses such a polymer. Right now, however, this chemical transistor is a mere curiosity.

Transistors, first introduced in 1947, are the heart and soul of modern electronics (a single silicon chip contains several such transistors). Wrighton's plastic transistor is smaller than a standard transistor, but unfortunately, it is much slower—a problem with all conducting polymers.

Wrighton's model takes 10 seconds to cycle on and then off. A silicon chip goes through the entire cycle in only a billionth of a second, a speed absolutely essential in modern electronics. Wrighton's chemical model is too slow to run a hand calculator, let alone a computer.

Still, given time, plastic transistors will probably find a place in our lives as have so many other plastic products.

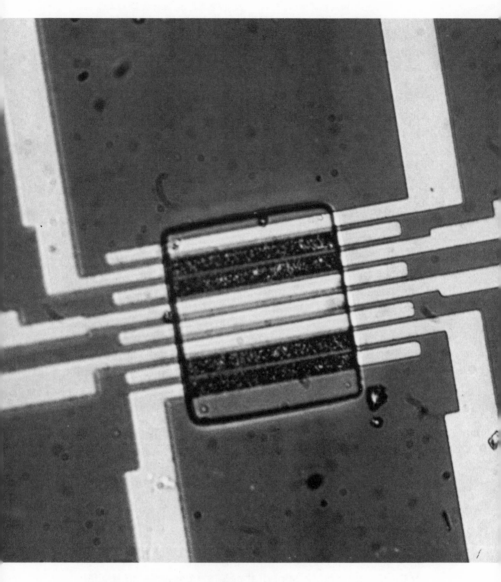

A plastic transistor (actually two).
Each pair of dark lines is one transistor.
The device is only 50 microns on a side
(1 micron is one-millionth of a meter; 1
millimeter is one-thousandth of a meter).

Obviously, no single commercial polymer is essential to our daily lives, but their very number has created a different world than that of fifty years ago. Because good, durable plastics are so inexpensive and so readily available for a multitude of uses, we have developed a casual acceptance of a life quite rich in material goods. Such an acceptance of our Plastic Age certainly has its problems, but few of us would give up our plastic goods. So, in its quiet way, this particular chemical revolution—the plastics revolution—has had an important impact on each and every one of us living in the last half of the twentieth century.

CHAPTER 4
PUTTING
THINGS
TOGETHER

*I*t is 1982, and J. D. Birchall and Anthony Kelly are testing a spring. They are pleased with their results. Under pressure, the coils compress normally, and when pulled apart and released, these same coils spring back into their resting state. The spring seems perfectly ordinary.

Except that it is made out of cement.

Birchall and Kelly are only two of the scientists involved in one of chemistry's most active revolutions: the replacement of older, conventional building materials, particularly metals, with synthetics. Whether chemistry can completely eliminate our need for steel and other structural metals is anyone's guess, but it certainly is working hard to reduce our metallic needs.

Why?

New plastics, ceramics, even cement have several advantages over metals. First, they are cheaper to make: The cement of Birchall and Kelly's spring takes 29 times less power to produce than steel. Second, these materials, particularly plastics, are easier to work, and in ratio to their weight, they are stronger than even steel. Finally, they resist corrosion better and, consequently, enjoy longer lives as parts of engines and industrial equipment.

HARD AS PLASTIC

When we think of plastic, we normally do not think of a substance that can be as strong, if not stronger (as we saw with Kevlar in the last chapter) than steel. Even today, in an age of plastic automobile bodies such as those on the Pontiac Fiero, we still often associate plastic with the word *cheap*.

This is an unfortunate connection, left over from early attempts to use plastic for jobs for which it was totally unsuited. Today's plastic is anything but cheap and unreliable.

For instance, Polimoter Research feels that the day of the plastic car engine is here. Their experimental racing car engine weighs 200 pounds (90 kilograms) less than all-metal engines. Less weight, less gasoline consumption. A car with such an engine will cost less to run.

Add this motor to a car built from DuPont's recently announced Rynite SST plastic, and the operating cost will be only 20 percent of a present-day car. DuPont feels its new plastic will hasten the replacement of metals since Rynite SST is twice as tough as previous plastics and is much less susceptible to damage from collisions than other structural plastics.

The testing of these new plastics has inspired the creation of machines such as that built by the Instron Corporation. Fully computerized, this instrument can test samples ranging from 6-inch (15-cm) squares to entire automobile bodies. It subjects the sample to temperatures running from −100° F (−38° C) to 4,000° F (2,200° C) and shoots a dart at 50 miles per hour (80 kilometers per hour) at the sample. It also puts the sample through a vigorous cycle of flexing and compression. This versatility allows researchers to discover if their newly designed plastic will do the job for which it was developed.

CUSHIONING THE BLOW

Where do these new plastics get their increased strength and durability? From the addition of glass or carbon. Almost all of these polymers are *composites.*

A composite has two parts. The first is a soft polymer, called a resin. Into this resin are embedded long fibers, known as whiskers. These whiskers are made by drawing carbon or glass out into long strings.

The two parts of the composite by themselves are not

A plastic-testing device used to evaluate various properties of polymers. Information obtained by subjecting a sample to various forces in the device on the left can be turned into graphs by the plotter on the right.

strong: The resin is soft, and any hard blow will crush it, while the whiskers are brittle and break easily. Together, however, the resin protects the whiskers from breaking by acting as a cushion, and the whiskers reinforce the resin, so that hard blows do not damage it.

Although not a composite, reinforced concrete works by the same principle because embedded iron rods keep the concrete from breaking and crumbling, while the concrete protects the rods from weather. It is so durable that a structure such as the Hoover Dam is stronger than some mountains.

The most famous modern composite is fiberglass, used to make insulating tape, fishing rods, and boat bodies. Made from a plastic such as polyester strengthened with glass whiskers, it is both flexible and light.

Strength combined with low weight have made composites among the most useful building materials of the 1980s. Being only 50 percent of the weight of steel and 25 percent of aluminum, composites have meant lighter airplanes with less fuel consumption. Aerospace companies use composites in building spacecraft such as the space shuttle and the Galileo probe, since the lighter the craft, the more practical it is to lift it off the surface of the earth.

One of the most important uses for composites is as artificial arms and legs. In the near future, these reinforced plastics will also be used to replace parts of diseased hearts and kidneys, as well as shattered bones and elbow and knee joints. Presently artificial hearts are made simply of polyurethane.

PITFALLS

It would be easy to give the impression that modern chemists with their knowledge of molecular structure have eliminated all problems. Decide what is needed, check the chemistry involved, and design the product.

It is not always so simple, as witnessed by the fact that metals are still very much in use. Chemistry still has its unknowns, as the Rolls-Royce Company discovered.

In the late 1960s, Rolls-Royce built a jet engine, in which it inserted fan blades made of a composite. The composite seemed as strong and as durable as the usual titanium metal blades, and they were considerably cheaper.

After the engine was in use, however, the company found that these composite blades broke off when hit by an object traveling at high speeds, such as a bird sucked into the engine intake. The end result was the replacement of the composite blades with the older titanium models.

So, despite our knowledge, there are still pitfalls. But these are the impetus for much of the continuing research in modern chemistry. If one thing does not work, investigate another.

TAKING THE HEAT

What do your family's china dinner plates, the tiles covering the space shuttles, power pole insulators, and bricks have in common? They are all *ceramics.* Normally, we associate the word ceramic with decorative figurines or the ashtray or pot we made during art class, but ceramics have been one of the most important building materials for humans since prehistoric times. And they continue to be, not so much replacing metals like plastic, but rather performing jobs that metals cannot.

All ceramics begin with clay—the same clay you can find along most river banks. This clay is a mixture of *oxides* of both silicon and aluminum; oxides are any compounds that have one or more elements bonded to oxygen. After the clay is worked into shape, it is baked until hard. Depending upon the exact composition of the clay, it can produce very delicate, fragile ceramics or tough, heat-resistant materials.

It is the latter products that have made ceramics a valuable building material. Few of us are not familiar with the heat-protective tiles that keep the shuttle from burning up on its return to earth from orbit. These tiles, feeling no heavier than balsa wood, are silicon oxide coated with a boron-silicon compound. They can take temperatures of up to 2,300° F (1,300° C) without melting.

This view of the space shuttle Columbia
shows the thermal protection tiles.

This shot of one of the space shuttles shows the protective tiles close up.

Already, however, W. Wheeler and his team at Lockheed Missiles and Space Company have developed a second-generation tile for the shuttle. These new tiles, tested during a shuttle mission in April 1984, have slightly different proportions of silicon oxide and boron-silicon coating, and they can withstand substantially higher temperatures than the older ones. In the 1984 test, they successfully replaced some of the older tiles that had melted on reentry.

Almost no metal could hold up at 2,200° F (1,200° C). Aluminum, out of which the shuttle's skin is made, melts at half this temperature, and the few metals that would not melt upon reentry are too heavy for the shuttle's engines to lift or too difficult to work.

Nor is the space shuttle the only place in which ceramics are proving their value over metal. The Cummins Engine Company has built for the U.S. Army an all-ceramic truck engine. Such an engine does not need any cooling system since the ceramic parts, unlike metal ones, are not bothered by the heat of operation. A 5-ton (4.5-metric-ton) truck, minus radiator, fan belt, and water pump, made a 500-mile (800-kilometer) trip with this ceramic engine. Because the engine was lighter than its all-metal counterpart, the truck got twice as much mileage per gallon as a conventional truck. The Kyocera Corporation of Japan is now testing a car with such an engine.

PACK 'EM IN

Before industrial ceramics can fully compete with metals, two problems must be solved. First, many ceramic pieces upon cooling take irregular shapes and must be machined, an expensive and time-consuming process. Second, ceramic pieces often develop small cracks; such flaws make them useless.

Industrial ceramics begin as particles that are fused together at high temperatures. These particles, however, are not all the same size, and as they pack down during fusion, they leave gaps. These gaps result in the irregular shrinking and the cracking.

John S. Haggerty of the MIT Energy Lab may have a solution to these gaps. Using a high-powered carbon-dioxide

A ceramic truck engine developed for the U.S. Army

*Three hundred thirty-eight pounds
(about 150 kilograms) of parts the
ceramic truck engine no longer needs!
Most are part of the cooling system,
which is no longer necessary.*

laser, Haggerty vaporizes the particles. As the particles recool, they solidify again, this time as uniform spheres.

Haggerty then suspends the ceramic spheres in a liquid and gives all of them a similar electric charge. As with like poles of magnets, the similarly charged spheres repel each other, and in doing so, create equal spacing between each sphere. Haggerty then removes the charge and evaporates the liquid; the spheres pack down into a gapless ceramic.

ON THE BOUNCE

Packing ceramic structure tighter is the secret of Birchall and Kelly's cement spring mentioned at the beginning of this chapter. Cement is a ceramic, but one with large and numerous pores (look at a cement wall).

Birchall and Kelly found that, by developing a new cement with very small pores, they had a cement flexible enough to make their spring. Their purpose in casting it as a spring was not necessarily to create a replacement for metal bedsprings and car suspension systems, but to show how tough and versatile their new product is.

Repeated testing showed no cracking in their porcelain-like spring. This new cement, called macro-defect free, is as strong as aluminum, and the two researchers plan to make it even stronger by adding reinforcing plastic fibers.

We cannot know the exact future of Birchall and Kelly's cement, but we can be sure that it, along with the many other new materials coming out of chemistry labs, will find a place in our world. Perhaps, in the near future, cement-bodied cars will join our cement sidewalks.

CHAPTER 5
HOT CHEMISTRY

THE PHILOSOPHER'S STONE

It is 1941, and three Harvard scientists anxiously wait for the test results. Sherr, Bainbridge, and Anderson are sure the experiment worked, and now they can check the test data and be sure. Yes, they have done it; they have changed mercury into gold. They have achieved the old alchemists' dream.

Medieval Europe was the last great age of the alchemists, who gave birth to modern chemistry. In turn, modern chemistry completed the quest of the alchemist: to find a way to make gold from some other, less valuable metal.

The alchemists were certain that some substance, known as the Philosopher's Stone, would change lead into gold. Did Sherr, Bainbridge, and Anderson have a Philosopher's Stone? Yes. The *nuclear reaction*.

In a nuclear reaction, an element changes into a completely different element—mercury into gold—but not through chemical action. Rather, the nuclei of that first element spontaneously undergo this change. For example, radium, atomic number 91, becomes radon, atomic number 86. Such a spontaneous change is *radioactive decay* and is accompanied by the release of charged *alpha particles*, *beta particles*, and *gamma rays*, known as *radiation*.

So far, our focus has been on the research and development of the chemical reaction. Chemists, however, also deal with the nuclear reaction. Their work with this has not only revolutionized chemistry, but the world. It is one of the major scientific revolutions of the twentieth century.

Even the early nuclear chemists recognized the potential value of radioactivity. First, it gave them clues as to the internal structure of the atom. Second, it promised to be a source of power, for radioactive decay produces heat and heat can be turned into electric power. Madame Curie, perhaps the most famous of these early researchers, noted that the decay of 1 gram (0.04 ounce) of radium produces in 4½ days as much energy as the burning of 1 gram of coal. Unlike that gram of coal, which is rapidly consumed, the gram of radium continues putting out energy for months, even years.

SPLITTING
THE ATOM

In 1938, the German scientists Otto Hahn and Fritz Strassmann achieved a major breakthrough that changed nuclear chemistry into one of the most important branches of chemistry. Hahn and Strassmann split the nucleus of a uranium atom (atomic number 92) into barium (atomic number 56) and krypton (atomic number 36) (notice the atomic numbers of barium and krypton add up to 92).

The two German scientists had performed *nuclear fission*—the splitting of an atomic nucleus into nuclei of atoms with smaller atomic numbers. Just as a billiard game begins with a player breaking the clustered balls with a cue ball, so fission begins with the scientist breaking the nuclear cluster of protons and neutrons by shooting a neutron into the atomic core.

As nuclear chemists continued studying the fission of uranium, they discovered that some kinds of uranium would release neutrons in their breakup, and that these neutrons would in turn shatter other uranium atoms. For every one of these uranium atoms split, two to three neutrons go flying, and the number of fissioning atoms quickly grows. This is the *chain reaction* (see Figure 5).

With a large enough amount (called the *critical mass*) of this chain-reacting uranium, you have a fission reaction that is self-sustaining. This means that, until all the uranium is

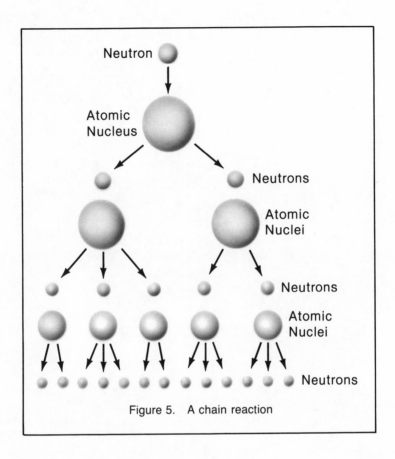

Figure 5. A chain reaction

split, the fission reaction continues, as does the heat it produces.

The self-sustaining fission reaction is the basis for both the atomic bomb and the nuclear power plant. The fission bomb violently shoves its nuclear material together in a fraction of a second to form the critical mass. The fission reaction proceeds so rapidly and releases such large amounts of energy that the end result is the nuclear explosion.

Unless the critical mass forms quickly, however, there is no explosion. Instead, there is the slow, steady production of heat from radioactive decay. This is the basis for the nuclear power plant. Whatever other dangers such plants may or

may not pose, a nuclear explosion is not one of them—it is a physical impossibility.

At the core of the nuclear power plant is the *nuclear reactor*, the sealed section of the plant in which the fission reaction occurs. Despite its completely twentieth-century core, such plants operate very much as do coal- or oil-generating plants. Steam drives a turbine that produces electricity.

Where other power plants get their steam from burning coal or oil, the nuclear power plant gets its from the heat of the fission reaction. The reaction converts water into steam that moves through a system that transfers the heat to a physically separate water supply. It is this which drives the plant's turbines.

THE VALUE OF THE ATOM

Power is by no means the only product of nuclear chemistry. The *radioactive tracer* is at least as important. Tracers are any radioactive material used to follow, that is, trace, everything from the course of chemical reactions to machine wear to oil flow. They have become important in medicine, particularly in locating diseased parts of the body.

Most tracers are *radioactive isotopes* of elements such as carbon or hydrogen. As we saw in chapter 2, all atoms of an element have the same atomic number, the same number of protons. However, the number of neutrons in these atoms may vary. When two atoms have the same number of protons, but a different number of neutrons, they are isotopes.

Carbon has three such isotopes, all of which have six protons in their nucleus. Carbon-12, the most common isotope, has six neutrons, but carbon-13 has seven neutrons

The High Flux Isotope Reactor at Oak Ridge National Laboratory in Tennessee is a key facility in the national program to produce and conduct research on manmade elements heavier than plutonium. Its principal product is the isotope californium-252.

and carbon-14 eight neutrons. Both carbon-13 and carbon-14 are radioactive isotopes of carbon.

Nuclear reactions are completely independent of chemical reactions. A radioactive element can be part of a molecule taking part in a chemical reaction, and the radioactive decay continues as usual. The chemical change also proceeds as though no radioactive element was present.

This is particularly important in medical diagnosis using tracers. For instance, the Positron Emission Transaxial Tomography (PETT) scanner looks for the location of brain tumors with the help of a radioactive tracer, tritium. Tritium, a hydrogen isotope, is part of a chemical compound.

After injection into a patient, this tritium-containing compound makes its way to the brain, where the most active sections draw the tracer to them. If there is a tumor, the tritium compound will end up in it. Then, through the detection of radioactive decay, doctors can locate and watch the tumor, as well as measure its size.

Tracers do not just help in medical diagnosis. Take an experimental automobile engine. The designers naturally want to know what type of wear the cylinder block and pistons experience. Is it serious, or is it acceptable in normal usage?

The diagnosis of wear begins with the placement of the piston rings either in a nuclear reactor or near a radioactive compound. After the metal becomes radioactive, technicians put the piston rings back into the engine. Then, running the engine, they check the oil for radioactivity. In this way, they can determine the amount of radioactive steel from piston wear.

Tracers are even used to separate various grades of oil. Although there are many grades of oil, each designed for different lubricating jobs, only one system of oil pipelines carries the oil across the country. Since the different grades are all sent through the same set of pipes, how do oil companies keep them separate?

At the point where one grade of oil ends and the next begins, the companies place a tracer. Radiation detectors, located along the inside of the pipeline, keep the flow moving in one direction until the tracer is detected. A new set of

*PETT scanner at Brookhaven
National Laboratory in New York.*

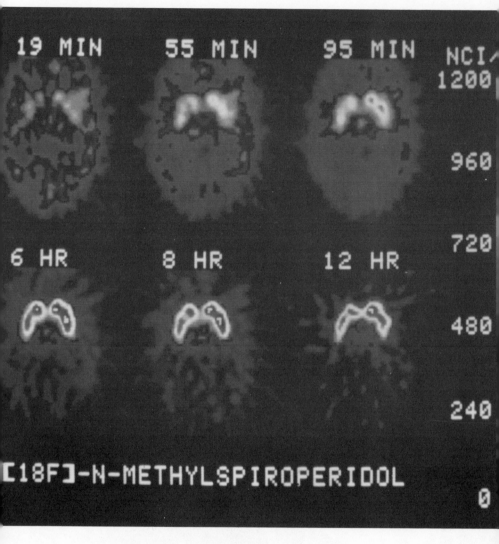

PETT brain scan of a normal subject. The scan shows the uptake of the radioactive tracer at different intervals of time. After twelve hours, the tracer is concentrated in one part of the brain.

valves is then opened, and the second grade of oil flows in a different direction from the first.

A DOSE OR TWO

Normally, we think of the radiation from nuclear reactions as dangerous, and it is, at least in large dosages. However, radiation does have its uses.

For example, radiation therapy has been an effective weapon against some cancers for almost forty years. Until recently, such therapy consisted of a narrow beam of gamma rays pumped into the cancerous growth. Since these cancer cells are more susceptible to radiation (they die more rapidly) than normal, healthy cells, such treatment often resulted in the destruction of part if not all of the cancer.

Within the last five years, doctors have begun using radioactive particles such as hydrogen nuclei and neutrons to replace gamma radiation treatments; even a narrow beam of gamma rays does damage some healthy tissue. Charged particles, however, do most of their damage at the target— the cancer cells—and seem to hurt normal cells less than gamma radiation.

THE HYDROGEN FUTURE

Although in the 1980s nuclear power plants and radioactive products are the result of controlled nuclear fission, a second nuclear process may present us with an alternative nuclear future. This is *nuclear fusion*, in which two atomic nuclei are forced—that is, fused—together to form a larger atom.

Ironically, scientists first performed nuclear fusion before nuclear fission. In the early 1930s, researchers forcefully shoved together a hydrogen atom and another of its radio-active isotopes, deuterium. Both hydrogen and deuterium are atomic number 1, but the product was helium, atomic number 2.

This fusion reaction released a great deal of energy, even greater than from a fission reaction. However, so much energy was required to force the atomic nuclei together that the net energy gain was zero. Nuclear fusion demands astronomically great temperatures, over 200 million° F (100 million° C).

Such a temperature rivals the temperature at the interior of the sun. Controlling a process that not only needs, but generates, such temperatures, poses special technical problems.

Does that mean that controlled fusion is a fantasy? No. It does mean that commercially controlled fusion is at least fifty years in the future.

Since the 1950s, a number of experimental projects have attempted to develop commercial fusion power. They all have to deal with ways to start the fusion reaction (some scientists think the answer is the laser) and then to contain the sunlike-reacting hydrogen. Containment is done by a magnetic field (see Figure 6), making the outside of the most recent experimental reactors look like large donuts.

Since the work is neither easy nor cheap, is it worth it? To some researchers, the answer appears to be yes. First, they point out the fuel for future fusion power plants would be the radioactive isotope of hydrogen, deuterium. This fuel would come from the sea, and although it makes up only 1½ percent of the ocean, there is enough deuterium to last several million years.

Second, these scientists calculate that, from the same amount of fuel, a fusion reactor would produce four times the energy of a fission plant. Additionally, they claim both the fuel and the radioactive by-products are much less dangerous than fission by-products such as plutonium since they are also easier to handle.

Perhaps best of all, these proponents insist since the fusion plant will require so little fuel at any one time, it diminishes the chance of accident. The fear of nuclear meltdown may become a thing of the past.

THE NEW ALCHEMY

While some nuclear scientists continue working to harness nuclear fusion, others investigate the process Sherr, Bainbridge, and Anderson used to change mercury into gold. To change one element into another is *transmutation*, and this

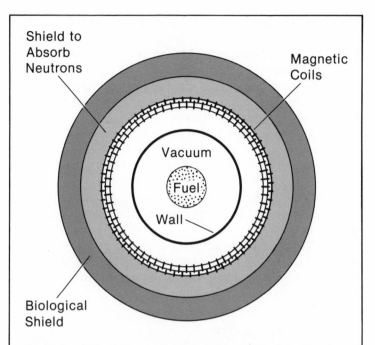

Figure 6. This cutaway view shows the major elements of a fusion reactor. First, at the reactor center, is a vacuum-sealed vessel holding the hydrogen fuel. Second, surrounding this core, are powerful magnetic coils that form a magnetic wall to contain the super-hot reacting fuel. Finally, there are two protective shields that prevent fusion-produced neutrons and radiation from escaping.

new alchemy created an entirely new field of chemistry—the study of the *transuranics*.

Transuranics are elements with atomic numbers higher than uranium's 92. Of these elements, the most famous is atomic number 94, plutonium, commonly used in nuclear reactors and atomic bombs. With the production of plutonium in 1942, chemistry had done more than just transmute one element into another. It had created an element that did not exist in nature, but then, none of the transuranics are found in nature.

All of the transuranics are radioactive, and if they ever existed naturally, they long since decayed into other elements. When created, any of these new elements lasts only seconds or fractions of a second.

Such short lives make identification of these elements difficult. The difficulty in studying transuranics does not end there. It takes time and energy to manufacture these elements. Glen Seaborg and Albert Ghiorso took three years to produce a mere two atoms of element 101. Elements 99 and 100 were produced in the explosion of the first hydrogen bomb.

In August 1982, a West German team headed by Peter Armbruster set out to create element 109. Using a powerful particle accelerator, they pushed iron atom nuclei (atomic number 26) to near the speed of light and then shot them at atoms of bismuth (atomic number 83). After ten full days of this, they may have—only may have—produced *one* atom of 109!

ISLANDS OF STABILITY

What started out as an almost random search for elements of higher and higher atomic numbers now has a goal. Nuclear chemists such as Albert Ghiorso wish to synthesize elements above 110, specifically 114 or 116. Why?

Current theory says that these elements, known as superheavy elements, are more stable. That is, unlike most of the known transuranics, they last longer than a few seconds. They form an island of stability among these transitory, new elements.

How long would such a superheavy element last? No one will know that until such an element is made. We can expect that their lives are not exceptionally long since none are found in nature; this absence argues that they have long ago spontaneously decayed. But even if they remain in existence only a matter of months or years, chemists would still have time to study and work with them.

Such superheavy elements may be similar to some of the common metals: 110 might be like platinum, 111 like gold, 114 like lead. They might even have commercial uses.

The Alternating Gradient Synchrotron—a particle accelerator—at Brookhaven National Laboratory. Particles are accelerated in the ring, shown here, and then studied.

The problem, of course, is making a superheavy element. Presently, the most feasible route seems to be the fusion of atomic nuclei of sufficient size to give the superheavy element—much in the manner of the 109 formation.

By fusing plutonium (atomic number 94) and calcium (number 20), chemists might produce 114. However, Peter Armbruster's West German team in cooperation with a U.S. group is investigating the production of 116 by fusing curium (number 96) with calcium. Element 116 would be well into this island of stability, if it exists at all, and could serve as the base for further superheavy element manufacture. Unfortunately, as of early 1985, Armbruster's efforts have failed to produce 116.

A DIFFERENT TYPE OF GOLD

The transuranics are not without their uses. They provide fuel for nuclear power stations and ships. Such installations and vessels cannot depend solely on the only natural occurring nuclear fuel, uranium-235. There is just not enough of it. Most of the naturally occurring uranium is uranium-238, which cannot sustain a chain reaction. Through transmutation, chemists are able to manufacture not only more uranium-235, but also uranium-233 and plutonium-239, which make excellent nuclear fuels.

Plutonium and other transuranics also supply the power in nuclear batteries. Weighing about 30 pounds (13.5 kilograms) and containing a small amount of nuclear material, such batteries provide power for untenanted lighthouses and navigation buoys. They were used in the Apollo spacecraft and are still generating electricity for many earth-orbit satellites since they have a ten-year lifetime.

Such nuclear-powered batteries have medical uses, too. They provide the life for *heart pacemakers*, electrical devices that keep irregularly beating hearts pumping steadily. Nuclear pacemakers outlast the older chemical models by a good eight years. By the late 1970s, some 2,000 atomic pacemakers were successfully in place.

Another transuranic, californium, element 98, is an excellent neutron source. If another nonradioactive element sits next to californium, the nonradioactive element converts into its radioactive isotope. If you need carbon-14, just place carbon-12 near a mass of californium and wait for the transuranic's escaping neutrons to make carbon-14. By creating the radioactive isotope where it is needed, you avoid losing part of it through radioactive decay as you transport it to the hospital or factory where it is needed.

Californium also presents doctors with a third method of applying radiation therapy to cancer patients. The doctor inserts small amounts of californium into the cancerous growth. The radiation from the transuranic is as deadly to the tumor as a tight beam of exterior radiation or projected radioactive particles. It, however, does not have to pass through the patient's healthy tissue to reach its goal. Further, since californium lasts only a short time, it disappears quickly after its job is done, keeping the radiation dosage to the patient down to a minimum.

Because of its short life, nuclear chemists have a difficult time manufacturing enough californium to last long enough to do its various jobs. At Oak Ridge, Tennessee, nuclear chemists are able to make small but significant amounts of this transuranic. They place uranium and plutonium in a fission reactor and then bombard them with a steady stream of neutrons. This method produces enough californium for commercial use.

The old alchemists were right. There is wealth in transmutation, but not from the creation of gold. Rather, the wealth is in the form of information and practical applications.

But perhaps most startling of all is the realization that this one branch of chemistry, nuclear chemistry, has helped alter an entire world. Whether we approve or not, the Atomic Age has given us devices and knowledge that were barely dreamed of at the turn of this century.

CHAPTER 6
THE CHEMICAL TOOL

As we have seen in the last few chapters, chemistry is a powerful tool for industry. It is also an important tool for other sciences, which make use of it to discover new knowledge, and revolutions in chemistry often are revolutions in other fields. Nor, as we shall see, is this tool confined merely to the sciences since even art and music find chemistry a useful instrument.

DOWN TO EARTH

On September 19, 1985, Mexico City rocked under a major earthquake. This one and a second one a day and a half later toppled apartment buildings and hospitals and shattered houses. Thousands of people, trapped in the ruins, died, and hundreds of buildings were completely destroyed.

As with all major earthquakes, the Mexican quake was a human disaster of epic proportions, and we can only wish that some way existed of warning people of impending earthquakes. Perhaps, if such a warning could be sounded in time, loss of life could be drastically cut.

Even as newspaper reporters and TV journalists zeroed in on the drama of rescue and recovery in Mexico City, chemists around the world quietly continued their search for a method of chemically detecting future quakes.

Geochemists—scientists who study the chemical nature of the earth—use this tool to probe for those chemical clues that can forewarn of earthquakes. These clues appear to be the same as those related to volcanic eruptions, and much of

Earthquake damage

the work has been actually done in volcanic regions of the world. So far, unfortunately, the results only hint at ways to forecast these events.

In early 1985, Kenneth A. McGee reported that eruptions and quakes seem to be preceded by the release of large amounts of hydrogen gas. Earthquake faults and volcanoes often release hydrogen gas, but normally only in small amounts. Prior to an eruption or a quake, this amount commonly rises to ten times its normal rate.

A week before the January 3, 1983, eruption of Mount Kilauea in Hawaii, McGee detected this sudden increase in hydrogen gas. The geochemist had similar results prior to eruptions of Mount St. Helens in Washington state and Mauna Loa in Hawaii.

As with other chemical tests for earthquakes and volcanic activity, McGee's is far from foolproof. On May 18, 1983, McGee detected a large release of hydrogen from an earthquake fault in California. According to the scientist's previous experiences, this should have meant a large quake on May 26. There was no quake then or ever in that area in 1983.

Such a failure does not mean that McGee's hydrogen gas cannot help in predicting earthquakes and volcanic eruptions. Rather, it means that forecasting such events will necessarily be done by putting together a number of clues; hydrogen release will only be one of these. Another is the release of radon, a radioactive gas, linked to both earthquakes and eruptions. And a third, according to Naoji Koizumi of Kyoto University in Japan, may be a rise in chlorine concentrations in mineral springs near earthquake faults. Koizumi, however, was unable to pinpoint the exact relationship between quakes and this increase in chlorine. Undaunted, McGee, Koizumi, and other geochemists continue searching for that still elusive chemical indicator, and with each observation and each experiment, they appear to be coming closer to discovering it.

TRACKING DOWN THE PAST

The geochemists's search is far from the only one using the chemical tool. In recent years, archaeologists have found chemistry invaluable in revealing the unwritten history of our ancestors.

For example, George Rapp of the University of Minnesota uses chemistry to trace the trade routes of North American Indians. He has been able to trace such routes for as long as 1,000 miles (1,600 kilometers). The record of these routes is in the copper many Indians employed for tools and jewelry, copper the Indians obtained by trading with other tribes.

This copper was far from pure and contained many contaminating chemicals, but the type of chemical contaminate varied from place to place. A copper lode in northern Minnesota would have a slightly different chemical makeup than one in central Minnesota or in Illinois or Wisconsin.

By taking a scraping from a piece of jewelry, Rapp can tell through chemical analysis where the copper originated. With enough such samples, he can plot the various trade paths from tribe to tribe. He can even tell when a lode in Minnesota finally ran out and trade shifted to a lode in Illinois.

While Rapp rediscovers old trade routes in North America, Thomas H. Lay, Associate Curator of the British Columbia Province Museum, finds out what the North Americans of 1,000 to 6,000 years ago hunted and ate. Normally, the prey of early hunters is obvious from the animal bones found in excavated camp sites. Sometimes, however, the bones have decomposed. Lay has found a way around this problem with chemistry.

Using a chemically coated strip, Lay tests samples of dried blood found on the stone tools and weapons of these early North Americans. The coated strip is the same one that hospitals use for quick blood analysis of emergency patients.

To date, Lay has found on these stone artifacts the blood of blacktailed deer, moose, snowshoe rabbits, California sea lions, and Stone Mountain sheep. He has also found human blood, but he believes this to be the blood of the tool and weapon makers, who occasionally must have cut themselves while fashioning these implements.

Other archaeologists use chemistry to investigate the possibility of Viking settlements in Newfoundland and Nova

Scotia. Although no one denies that Vikings visited North America in the tenth century A.D., archaeologists have never been too certain if any of these Scandinavian rovers stayed and attempted to settle. Several tentative settlement sites have been discovered, but whether they were only temporary winter camps or something more permanent has been difficult to determine.

Searchers have discovered several tools, definitely of Viking origin, at some of these sites. Chemical analysis of the composition of these tools showed that the source of the material was from farther north. The archaeologist can conclude that at least some Vikings spent enough time in North America to work their way south.

Did they stay at this spot for any length of time? Long enough to make tools out of local substances, an observation supported again by chemistry. These particular Vikings did settle these sites for at least a few years.

SECRET OF THE PYRAMIDS?

Joseph Davidovits, a chemist at Barry University, Miami, Florida, believes he has discovered how the Egyptian pyramids were constructed.

Traditionally, historians and anthropologists have described the building of these pyramids as a lifetime of labor by thousands of sweating slaves. Each block was supposedly dragged miles from its quarry and then wrestled up large ramps into a designated place in the growing pyramid.

Davidovits, however, thinks the blocks were cast in place. Workers at the quarries ground up the limestone, which was then mixed with water. Other workers poured this mixture into large molds at the construction site. Into the mold, they also added a chemical which hardened the limestone solution.

As proof of his theory, Davidovits offers the chemical composition of the actual pyramid blocks. First, their composition is different from the stone of nearby quarries, a difference accountable by Davidovits's proposed method of preparation. Second, these blocks contain by weight 13 percent

The Egyptian pyramids may have
been built from water, ground
limestone, and a chemical that
hardened the solution.

of a chemical that could be the hardener used in the limestone mixture.

If Davidovits's theory is correct, the building of the pyramids required a much shorter period of time and a much smaller work force than previously suspected. Time and chemistry will tell.

DATING THE PAST

Probably chemistry's most important role in archaeology is providing a way to date ancient tools, art, weapons, clothing, even preserved food. The most famous of these chemical dating methods is carbon-14 dating, developed by the American chemist Willard Libby in the 1940s.

Carbon-14 is a radioactive isotope of carbon-12 and is found in detectable, although incredibly tiny, amounts in any artifact made from plant or animal tissue, particularly cloth fibers. As with all radioactive material, carbon-14 breaks down into other elements over time. In 5,730 years, half of any amount of carbon-14 is gone, converted into another element. This period is known as the *half-life*.

Take a kilogram (2.2 pounds) of carbon-14. After 5,730 years, it will have dwindled to half a kilogram (1.1 pounds); the other half kilogram is now nitrogen-14. After another 5,730 years, it will be a quarter of a kilogram (0.55 pound), and so on, until nothing is left of that kilogram of carbon-14.

By discovering the percentage of carbon-14 and knowing its half-life, an archaeologist can determine the age of, say, a wooden carving or a woven mat. Unfortunately, such dating is not exact: You can tell within a few centuries, but you cannot tell to the year how old something is. Obviously this is not a good system to use on objects from the recent past.

The problem comes from a variation in the amount of carbon-14 in the atmosphere from year to year. Since no one can know how much of this isotope was present in any particular year in the past, there is no way to compensate for this fluctuation.

Still, we know from carbon-14 dating that the Lascaux charcoal cave paintings in France are 15,516 years old plus or minus 900 years. Wheat and barley from ancient Egypt are 6,095 years old plus or minus 250 years. The linen wrapping around the Dead Sea Scrolls is 1,917 years old plus or minus 200.

Carbon-14 dating is not the only such system available to archaeologists. It is merely the oldest and one of the most reliable.

CHEMICAL ART

Chemistry is also helping to save and in some cases restore both artifacts and art objects. Using various polymers, archaeologists have begun preserving objects as old as 10,000 years—the end of the last Ice Age. The technique requires that the object be thoroughly saturated with the polymer, which then keeps it from crumbling away. To date, chemists have treated an old Egyptian wood yoke with such a polymer, and they may eventually use this method to save what is left of the Parthenon in Athens, whose stone is being eaten away by air pollution.

A nylon polymer is now available for preservation work. It forms a protective coat and so far has saved flaking paintings in Egyptian tombs, crumbling illuminated medieval manuscripts, and disintegrating fabrics.

Art museums have also found chemistry a useful tool in evaluating paintings, sculptures, and other artwork. Through chemical analysis, Leanna Whitman of the Winterthur Museum has been able to differentiate between eighteenth-century Chinese and European painted silks.

Whitman exposed the silks to X-rays, which cause the various paints to glow or fluoresce. Each paint has its own unique fluorescence.

From such an analysis, Whitman has discovered that Chinese silks have leaves and flowers outlined with silver-based paint, while their browns come from an iron pigment. European silks, however, were painted using non-metallic-based paints. From these chemically different paints, Whitman and others can tell, when there is doubt, whether a painted silk is Chinese or European.

A Stradivarius violin, made in Cremona, Italy, in 1694. For years, people have been trying to discover the "secret ingredient" of Antonio Stradivari's magnificent instruments.

VIOLIN CHEMISTRY

Upon his death in 1737, Antonio Stradivari left the world 1,500 of the finest violins ever made. In the succeeding centuries, no one was able to discover the secret that gave these instruments such an excellent sound. Now, 250 years after Stradivari's death, Joseph Nagyvary, a Texas A&M chemist, may have the answer—a chemical answer.

Nagyvary is convinced that Stradivari's secret was in the chemicals the violin maker used to treat the wood out of which he built his violins. Nagyvary has developed his own chemical wood treatments as well as varnish in hopes of reproducing the sound of these 250-year-old violins.

In 1984, the Landolfi String Quartet of St. Louis played half their concert with Nagyvary's violins. The verdict? Both the players and music critics applauded Nagyvary's instruments.

Chemistry is a versatile tool. Even in such disciplines as music and art, normally not associated with the sciences, chemistry has created possibilities where no possibilities previously existed.

CHAPTER 7
THE SAND
CONNECTION

Sand. Anyone who has been to a beach has picked up a handful and let it sift through his or her fingers. Normally, we think no more of it than how pleasant it feels under the warm summer sun.

Yet that handful of sand contains one of the most important chemical elements of the twentieth century: silicon. We are all familiar with the word "silicon." We know of it because of Silicon Valley and the silicon chip, and we know of these because of news stories, books, and movies.

What is silicon? Next to oxygen, it is the most abundant chemical element in the earth's crust, making up some 28 percent. It has also provided the base for a number of chemical revolutions from glass making to electronic component manufacturing.

THROUGH A GLASS . . .

Anything as common as silicon must have found its way into human life before the twentieth century. Indeed, the history of one silicon product, glass, is at least 4,000 years old. The twentieth-century chemist, however, has not neglected taking a good look at glass, particularly glass manufacturing.

One of the major steps in glass production is heating its starting components to some 2,000° F (1,100° C). It takes special equipment to handle any substance this hot, adding both to the expense and the difficulty in making glass.

The search is on, therefore, for a cool process to manufacture glass, and Larry Hensch of the University of Florida may have discovered just such a process. Hensch has developed a silicon mixture that forms a jellylike material, which can be baked at just a few hundred degrees Fahrenheit to become glass. If Hensch's method proves economically feasible, it will have several advantages over old glassmaking ways.

First, it will allow for a better-quality glass since the chemicals in glass mix more uniformly at low temperatures than high. Such high-quality glass will benefit astronomers since telescope mirrors will no longer take years to finish, but rather days or weeks. Better glass is in demand for lenses for laser systems and for fiber optics. Fiber optics, thin rods of glass that transmit light even around curves, are becoming important to communication since information can be sent through them in the form of coded light pulses.

Second, molded glass will become a much more important product than it is now. Presently, the best glass is blown glass. Watching a glass maker turn a gob of molten glass into a bottle or bowl by blowing in controlled breaths through a long tube is spectacular. This process, however, is an art, taking a great deal of skill, and does not lend itself to mass-produced, high-quality glass products. Only molds can provide such mass production.

Contemporary molded glass does exist but is expensive since it requires costly high-temperature molds to cast the glass. With low-temperature glass, inexpensive plastic molds, which would melt if 2,000° F (1,100° C) glass were poured into them, would be practical.

TO BUILD A NEW CHAIN

Beyond its uses in glassmaking, silicon interests chemists because it is a close chemical relative of carbon. Like carbon, the silicon atom can bond to as many as four other atoms, and it forms similar compounds. Where carbon and oxygen become carbon dioxide, silicon and oxygen become silicon dioxide.

As we have seen, carbon's ability to form long chains of carbon atoms (polymers) has made it valuable to modern chemistry. The natural question for any chemist is whether silicon atoms can form similar chains, forming silicon polymers. The answer is no, not by itself.

Silicon is a larger atom than carbon, and consequently its bonds are not quite so stable. As a result, silicon cannot bond with itself to make long molecular chains.

In 1941, however, Eugene Rochow produced silicon polymers, which were a little different from carbon polymers. Rochow had been working with the chemistry of silicon and oxygen and discovered that long chains, consisting of alternating atoms of the two elements, not only were possible but made for stable compounds. These were the first *silicones.*

Within two years of Rochow's work, Dow Chemical and Corning Glass were marketing a line of these compounds, used to make rubber, lubricants, and plastics. Later, silicones would go into skin lotion, toothpaste, and car wax.

Since silicones do not react with oxygen in the air and can stand extreme heat and cold, they have proven invaluable as rubber gaskets and fittings as well as all-weather oils for airplanes. The modern plane carries about half a ton (450 kilograms) of silicones to keep its various hydraulic systems operating and to ensure that its electrical wiring is soundly insulated.

Silicones are also water resistant and have become a major waterproofing substance. In waterproofing ceramics, paper, or clothing fibers, workers first coat the material with a layer of water and then expose it to silicone vapor. The result is a protective covering of silicone.

Perhaps as important as anything are the medical uses of silicones. As a plastic, they make excellent artificial body parts.

Living matter is made up of carbon-based chemicals such as proteins and DNA. Human bodies, as with any living organisms, are geared to reject any foreign carbon-containing matter. This is part of our disease-fighting mechanism that allows our bodies to fight and kill invading microorganisms. Unfortunately, the system is unable to differentiate between these invaders and medical aids such as artificial heart valves. A carbon-based plastic will often be just as firmly rejected by the human body as a deadly bacterium.

Silicone plastics do not suffer this rejection trouble. Since

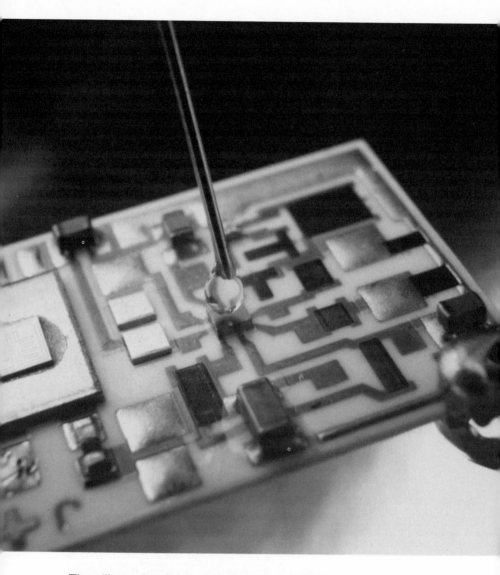

The silicon chip (center) is about to be "blob coated" with a high-purity silicone coating to protect it from dust, moisture, stress, and other factors that might mar its performance. The chip contains an integrated circuit.

they are not made from carbon, they do not trigger the body's immune system.

Without silicones, most of the implants designed and used by doctors would be impossible (although artificial hearts are still made of the carbon plastic polyurethane). For instance, some human babies are plagued by a fluid buildup in their brains. Normally such fluids drain off by themselves, but in a few cases, the natural valves do not work. To correct this problem, doctors insert a device through the brain tissue, muscle, bone, and skin of the baby to siphon off this liquid. A carbon-plastic construct quickly fails, but the silicones do not. They have been so successful that, by the end of the 1970s, over 50,000 of these devices were in use.

THE CHIP

The room *is* clean. It has less than 100 grains of dust per cubic foot (0.03 cubic meter). In it, men and women work quietly, completely covered from head to foot in white, protective clothing. The clothing is not to protect the workers, but to protect that on which they work. These people are making silicon chips, and even one dust mote lodging on one of these super-thin wafers can ruin hours of work.

Such production rooms are at the heart of the modern electronics industry. From them flow the components—the silicon chips—that run everything from digital wristwatches to personal computers. All of this exists because, under certain conditions, silicon conducts electricity.

We all know that electricity will move through some materials and not others. Those substances that will carry electricity, such as copper, aluminum, and other metals, are conductors, while those substances that will not carry electricity, such as rubber and most plastics, are insulators.

Silicon is neither; it is a *semiconductor*. Semiconductors are materials that at room temperature carry electricity better than insulators, but not nearly as well as conductors.

You might wonder what good a semiconductor is since it does not do either job well. If this were all there was to it, the semiconductor would be of academic interest only. Through the addition of other chemicals, however, semiconductors become excellent conductors. It was this discovery that led in 1948 to William Shockley, John Bardeen, and Walter Brattain's invention of the transistor. It was the first step toward the silicon chip.

Prior to 1948, the control and amplification of current in electronic equipment such as radio transmitters and radar required large, bulky vacuum tubes. These ranged from one inch to several inches in size.

Large equipment was run by a roomful of such tubes plus circuitry. The first computer, ENIAC, put into operation in 1946, weighed 30 tons (27 metric tons), used 18,000 vacuum tubes, and drew enough power to light a small town.

The *transistor* miniaturized all of this. The vacuum tubes quickly disappeared, and in their place were these new components measuring no more than half an inch (1.3 centimeters). Inside each transistor were two semiconductors placed together; chemical additives enhanced conductivity.

Like the vacuum tube, the transistor was merely a unit plugged into an electrical circuit. In the 1960s, researchers realized that, by using pieces of silicon, they could make the transistors and the circuit all one unit, called an *integrated circuit*. This reduced the circuitry even further, packing several thousand transistors on a silicon chip no more than 1/16 inch (1.6 millimeters) across. The most recent reduction has produced very-large-scale integrated circuits that hold 200,000 transistors (*one* of these can do more calculations than the old ENIAC and costs 30,000 times less to build).

To make a silicon chip is a tedious process. Workers in clean rooms chemically etch the circuits and transistors into the surface of the silicon chip. Part of the process involves laying down a polymer screen on top of a silicon wafer (each wafer is eventually cut into hundreds of chips). This screen allows the worker to etch out the circuit lines just like someone tracing letters of the alphabet with the help of a stencil.

The use of this polymer screen, though necessary, is one of the bottlenecks in silicon chip production. A. Wayne Johnson at Sandia National Laboratories has developed a possible way of eliminating this screen and speeding up chip

*A computer chip and the tip of a pencil.
The chip is about one-quarter inch
(6 millimeters) on a side.*

production. Johnson places a silicon wafer into a sealed chamber, which he then pumps full of the chemical compound that will form the circuits and transistors. An ultraviolet laser hits the wafer, and as it does, it lays down the suspended chemical compound in the desired circuit arrangements. Such a process would allow university and research labs to design and build their own specialized silicon chips.

NO RESISTANCE

There can be no question of the importance of silicon as a semiconductor, and there can be little doubt that it will remain an important part of the electronics industry for the conceivable future. It may, however, have another electrical role, that of *superconductor*.

A superconductor is the perfect conductor, having no resistance whatever to electricity. The first commercial superconductor, a metallic alloy, was produced in 1962 by Super Con. Since then several others have come on the market.

To date, superconductors have been used primarily to generate very large magnetic fields (all electric currents generate magnetic fields) for experimental fusion reactors and for high-energy particle accelerators. Ordinary conductors are unable to create magnetic fields anywhere near as strong.

The major drawback to more extensive use of superconductors, which could make for faster computers and more efficient engines, is the temperatures at which they operate: −416° F (−249° C). The search then is on for superconductors that operate at higher temperatures. Is silicon this superconductor? Perhaps.

For some years, theory said that silicon under intense pressure should become a superconductor. In March 1985, Michael M. Darorogna and colleagues at the University of California, Berkeley, were able to squeeze a sample of silicon between two diamond anvils until its atomic structure altered. The result was a superconductor. Unfortunately, it did not function as such except at −427° F (−255° C). The investigation of silicon's superconductivity, however, has only begun, and it may still reveal silicon to be that long-sought, high-temperature superconductor.

A POCKETFUL
OF MACHINES

Electrical engineer James B. Angell of Stanford University has decided that there is no reason to connect silicon chips to various instruments and machines. Instead, Angell builds the machine components onto a silicon chip—a new meaning to integrated circuit.

To date, this engineer has built nozzles to control ink jets on printers, small electrodes to monitor brain activity, and a miniature gas chromatography column. Their process of construction is the same as for making the normal electronic chips, but in this case, the chemical etching also adds various parts of the built-in instrument. These machine-chips are less prone to mechanical failure than their larger cousins.

The gas chromatography column rests on a silicon chip about the size of a box of matches. The column itself is 60 inches (1.5 meters) long and is wound tightly, looking much like a coil of rope, on the chip. Lab models of such columns stand 100 feet (30 meters) high, but Angell's miniature column works well as a portable unit for testing air quality in factories and mines and checking the contents in a natural gas pipeline.

Angell's silicon machine-chips may be of interest at the moment to those with specialized jobs, but the day may come when they are as much of a household item as other silicon products. Remember the importance of silicon the next time you work math problems with your pocket calculator.

CHAPTER 8
REAPING
A CHEMICAL
HARVEST

Aerobics. Running. Swimming. Lifting weights. These and other activities are all part of the health and fitness craze that has swept not only the U.S. but much of the rest of the world in the last fifteen years. Many people today are vitally concerned with their health as seen in the popularity of health food stores.

But this growing interest in health is also reflected in a chemical revolution in the manufacturing of drugs and the growing and processing of food. *Biochemists*, chemists concerned with the chemistry of living things, have been active in these areas for decades, but there is an increasing awareness among them, particularly in food processing, that their work is only just beginning and that new chemical knowledge means new approaches to good health.

TO FIND A
BETTER DRUG

Through 1985, the U.S. space shuttles made regular trips into orbit. In addition to carrying various communication and weather satellites, the shuttles provide space platforms for many scientific experiments aimed at discovering more about our planet, solar system, and universe.

Some of these experiments, however, have a much smaller focus: the analysis of molecular structure. Such exploration is only the most recent attempt by the *pharmaceutical industry* to find new and effective drugs against human disease.

The pharmaceutical industry has benefited as much as, if not more than, other industries from advances in chemical instrumentation and analysis and from increasing knowledge of molecular structure. Four out of every five drugs available in the 1980s were unknown fifty years ago, a time when the number of fatalities from serious disease was the same as in the previous century.

Now we live in a world that has completely eliminated one such disease, smallpox, and virtually wiped out another, tuberculosis—two of the greatest killers in human history. Doctors have been able to control many infections with penicillin and other antibiotics, and each of us has access to non-prescription painkillers such as aspirin and Advil. There are pharmaceuticals to control partially or fully such disorders as high blood pressure, allergies, and diabetes.

NOT ANOTHER COLD

Despite the progress that drug research has made in the past half century, no one would claim that we have all the drugs we need. Many diseases prove difficult to cure, let alone eliminate. One of the most common and certainly one of the most difficult to stamp out is the common cold.

The cause of colds are viruses—a *virus* is a microorganism—and because there are several hundred different cold viruses, the search for a single cure is complicated. Often a possible drug against one cold virus has proven ineffective against any other.

Guy Diana of Sterling-Winthrop Research Institute and his research group may have finally found that elusive cold cure. Diana's team announced in the spring of 1985 that they were testing a drug, WIN 51,711, which has killed off most of the test cold viruses in human-tissue cultures. It will, however, be several years before this drug can appear on store shelves since it has eighty more tests to pass, including those to see if it is toxic to humans.

Until WIN 51,711 is approved, we will probably have to be content with keeping other people from catching our cold. Kimberly-Clark has a new tissue called Avert. Each tissue is treated with a chemical that prevents cold viruses from spreading. A cold sufferer using Avert, therefore, protects those around him or her from the same discomfort.

DESIGNER DRUGS

With the advent of computer-simulated molecular structures in the early 1980s, biochemists began trying to custom-design drugs to meet specific needs. Even with computer assistance, this effort has been difficult since the molecules that make up most drugs are composed of hundreds of thousands of atoms. They are very complicated, and a mistake in their computer representation means the drug will not work. Out of every 8,000 molecules tested, only one proves an effective drug.

Work aboard the space shuttle may improve drug designing. In space, these molecules reach much larger sizes than on earth. During the Spacelab-1 shuttle flight, the West German astronaut Walter Littke produced a protein 1,000 times larger than its counterpart on earth. Weightlessness has profound effects on the growth of these complex molecules.

By using X-ray spectrometers, chemists can more easily determine the structure of these supergiant molecules from space. The structure is the same as if they had been produced here, but there is so much more of it that these giant proteins are much easier to analyze.

Such structural knowledge of specific drugs is particularly useful in learning how to avoid interference in drug therapy from the body's natural chemical compounds. Charles Rugg of the University of Alabama-Birmingham will have astronauts growing large samples of PNP, a protein found in human red blood cells. PNP's normal role is to chop up the chemical building blocks of the genetic material, DNA. PNP also chops up certain cancer treatment drugs, which it mistakes for those same DNA parts. Rugg hopes that with a large enough PNP, he can find out its structure and then design a compound that will temporarily stop the PNP long enough for the cancer drug to work.

SPACE DRUG

The shuttle is not only proving an excellent place to study molecular structure, but it is making an excellent factory for drug production. During a 1984 shuttle mission, Charles Walker of Johnson & Johnson's Ortho Pharmaceutical Company manufactured a new drug to treat diabetes.

The important step in the creation of this drug is its electrical separation from a mixture of other chemical compounds. The weightless conditions found in orbit aid this process, and the end product, the diabetes drug, is purer than if separated under earthly conditions, if it could be separated out at all.

FOOD BOOSTERS

We normally turn to drugs when we are ill, but we are taught early that a good diet is one of the keys to maintaining good health. That means we need certain foods in certain proportions. Prior to the twentieth century, most people either hunted, gathered, or raised their own food. However, in the U.S. and other developed countries, most people are dependent on store-bought food. Such food had to be transported and stored, often for long periods of time, and this meant that there have to be ways to keep it from spoiling. It was the creation of these necessary methods of preservation that has partially allowed (although not to everyone's satisfaction) the extent of urban growth in this and other countries. And this urban revolution was permitted by chemistry since chemical methods have been and still are one of the primary preservative techniques.

Biochemists did more, however, than just preserve food; they increased—boosted—its nutritional value. One of the important chemical discoveries prior to World War II was the need in the human diet for small amounts of chemicals called vitamins and trace elements. *Vitamins*, whose existence was not even suspected before the discovery of vitamin B_2 by the German biochemist Otto Warburg in the 1930s, are nitrogen-containing compounds that regulate the use of the chemicals we get from our food. For instance, vitamin D helps build bones from calcium and phosphorus. Vitamin C in orange

Astronaut Charles Walker, who manufactured
a drug on a space shuttle mission in 1984

juice keeps us from contracting scurvy, a disease character-ized by bleeding gums.

Trace elements are any chemical element that we need in small amounts to sustain our bodies. Iron is such a trace ele-ment. Without it, we become anemic and our blood is unable to carry enough oxygen to all parts of our bodies.

The discovery of vitamins and trace elements was impor-tant in giving researchers a clearer and more complete pic-ture of the human diet. It revealed the complexities of that diet: No longer was just a proper balance of proteins, sugars, and fats satisfactory for health. Incredibly small amounts of chemicals were of equal importance. According to recent findings by Leslie Kievav of the U.S. Department of Agricul-ture, each of us needs a mere 2 to 3 milligrams (0.00007 to 0.0001 ounce) of copper per day. Without it, we run the risk of anemia, weak bones, and heart problems.

The need for vitamins and trace elements eventually increased the role of chemistry in food processing beyond preservation. To insure that food had the necessary nutrients, chemists added them during processing. At the time, in the early 1940s, it was a revolutionary idea to chem-ically treat food in an attempt to promote good health. The practice has become so universal that few of us bother to read the list of vitamins and trace elements listed as supple-ments or *food additives* on the side of food packages.

Was this revolution in food preparation necessary? At least to some extent, yes. Modern food processing such as milk pasteurization destroys much of food's natural nu-trients. Food additives restore this nutrition. In other cases such as vitamin D in milk or iodine in salt, the additives are important substances not naturally present in a particular food. In the past, groups of people found themselves suffer-ing from a dietary deficiency because some vitamin or trace element was not in the food naturally available to them. Inland diets were often short on iodine, which is found most commonly in saltwater fish.

PROBLEMS IN ADDITION

But if chemistry appeared to solve a problem by discovering and then adding vitamins and trace elements to food, it also found problems with such additives. One class of additives, sweeteners, has proven to be a true problem.

Artificial sweeteners arose from a small revolution that was basically a good idea: Replace common table sugar. This sugar, which even today is found in large amounts in most foods as both sweetener and preservative, causes weight problems and tooth decay. The answer seemed logical: Find a synthetic substitute.

And chemists did. Unfortunately, all of these sweeteners from the oldest, saccharine, to the newest, aspartame, known as NutraSweet, have been attacked as possible causes of cancer and brain tumors.

The evidence is far from conclusive on this matter, but chemists have begun looking now for new sweeteners that will not only be superior to table sugar but also to the present-day synthetics. One such candidate has arrived in the chemistry lab courtesy of a sixteenth-century Spanish physician.

Francisco Hernándes visited Mexico not long after Cortez's conquest of the Aztecs and recorded in his journal information about a plant known to the Aztecs as a "sweet plant." In 1984, A. Douglas Kinghorn and Caesar M. Compadre of the University of Illinois Medical Center, using this sixteenth-century reference, tracked down this plant in the hopes of finding a natural sugar substitute.

Back in their lab, the two researchers isolated a colorless oil that proved to be 1,000 times sweeter than sugar. So far, it has passed initial tests showing that it does not cause cancer or tooth decay.

DOWN ON THE FARM

The chemical treatment of food begins even before it is harvested. One of the major revolutions in agricultural chemistry was the introduction of *pesticides*, chemicals that kill insect pests. Pesticides considerably increased crop yields, particularly for corn and soybeans. They also have become the center of controversy because of their possible ill effects upon human health as well as the environment.

Several of these chemicals, such as DDT and most recently ethylene dibromide, have been banned by the U.S.

The ''sweet plant''

*Aerial application of pesticide (crop dusting)
on alfalfa in western Colorado*

Food and Drug Administration. In the near future, other pesticides will undoubtedly join these two on the list of banned chemicals.

This chemical revolution is obviously in trouble, and biochemists have begun a chemical search for a solution that will give farmers a safe method of pest control. That method seems to be to find natural pesticides, that is, chemicals already in nature that can control insects.

James Nathanson of Harvard Medical School believes that caffeine, the stimulant in both coffee and cola drinks, may be such a natural pesticide. Nathanson tested the effect of caffeine on tobacco hornworm caterpillars. Repeated exposure stunted this caterpillar's growth and increased its death rate. Nathanson then sprayed tomato leaves with caffeine, cutting down significantly on insect damage.

At Washington State University, Clarence A. Ryan has isolated a chemical common to alfalfa, tomato, and potato plants. This chemical causes an insect's digestive system to shut down, so the insect literally starves to death. Since heat destroys this chemical, cooking makes plants safe for human consumption after being sprayed with this pesticide.

A third possible natural pesticide comes from the sea. Three University of Cairo chemists, Mahmoud Abbas Saleh, Nadia M. Abdel-Moein, and Nagy A. Ibrahim, have found that brown algae from the sea when air-dried for several days repel houseflies. The three scientists later isolated the essential chemical from the algae. In addition to the houseflies, this plant pesticide drove off rice weevils and cotton leaf worms.

To find out what we need to stay healthy and to keep us that way is one of the important products of much biochemical research, whether it is in developing new drugs, enhancing the nutrition of our food, or seeing that the process of growing our food does no harm. In some cases, the chemists have had to find chemical solutions to problems created by their initial chemical efforts.

As we shall see in the next chapter, such chemical threats are being exposed and fought in more than just this one area of chemistry.

CHAPTER 9
THE CHEMICAL HAZARD

IT'S IN THE AIR

Over 500 years old, the buildings in Colorado's Mesa Verde National Park are disappearing under the assault of wind, dust, and rain. But something else is at work here besides these natural elements. It eats away at the sandstone blocks fashioned by the Anasazi Indians. It is the same something eating away at marble statues in Washington, D.C., brick buildings in New York City, and ancient Roman and Greek monuments in Europe.

It is chemical pollution in the air.

Chemical pollution of the air, soil, and water is one of the major problems of the last half of the twentieth century, and the success of cleanup and control devices, such as the catalytic converter that changes the pollutants carbon monoxide and nitric oxide into carbon dioxide and nitrogen (see Figure 7) have been indifferent.

There are reasons for these failures. For one, in the U.S. alone, over 60,000 chemicals are now in use, and to these, each year adds another 1,000. According to the National Research Council (NRC), no one has tested 70 percent of these for toxicity. Although the NRC recommends that immediate testing begin on these chemicals, the job will take years, probably decades.

Additionally, the chemistry of pollution is poorly understood. Until 1983 and the work of Dr. Stephen J. Harris, no chemist could tell you much about the formation of soot (black carbon particles produced by combustion). Harris discovered that the size of soot particles depends on the presence of a specific chemical, acetylene, in the burning materials. This finding may be the first step in developing an effective control for a pollution problem that has plagued the industrial world since the last century.

AT THE EDGE OF SPACE

Although many of the pollutants that enter the air return to the Earth, some migrate up into the upper atmosphere. *Chlorofluorocarbons* (CFCs)—gases used as coolants in refrigerators and air conditioners—are perhaps the most serious of these upper-air pollutants. The major impact of CFCs is their destruction of *ozone*, a molecule having three oxygen atoms. Ozone forms a layer in the upper atmosphere that prevents us from receiving too much solar radiation. Loss of this layer could mean an increase in skin cancer as well as climatic changes.

How dangerous are CFCs to the ozone layer? In 1979, researchers were convinced that by the end of the century 16.5 percent of this layer would be gone, but a 1984 NRC report reduces that to only 4 percent. The difference arises because no one understands the chemistry of the atmosphere at all.

For example, subsonic airplanes may, in burning fuel, be adding ozone to the lower atmosphere. This ozone may be

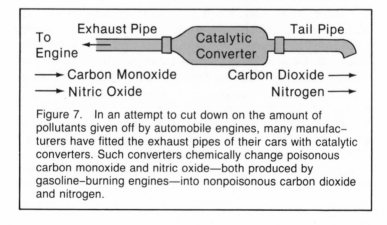

Figure 7. In an attempt to cut down on the amount of pollutants given off by automobile engines, many manufacturers have fitted the exhaust pipes of their cars with catalytic converters. Such converters chemically change poisonous carbon monoxide and nitric oxide—both produced by gasoline–burning engines—into nonpoisonous carbon dioxide and nitrogen.

itself migrating upward to resupply the ozone layer. This is, however, pure conjecture.

Because of such uncertainty and the importance of knowing what chemical pollution is doing to our planet's atmosphere, the National Academy of Science has launched an ambitious twenty-year program to study the chemistry of the atmosphere. They hope to learn enough to provide sound information on atmospheric pollution as well as how it should and can be handled.

TOO DANGEROUS TO BURY

The streets are deserted, not even a stray dog or cat visible. The storefronts are boarded up. The windows of the houses reveal empty, dusty rooms.

This is Times Beach, Missouri, and no one lives there anymore; now it is the property of the federal government. It is the town in which the Environmental Protection Agency (EPA) discovered such high levels of *dioxin* in the soil that they had no choice but to move the entire population for its own safety.

Experts consider dioxin, found in some herbicides, to be one of the most dangerous chemicals loose in our environment—only a few molecules of dioxin pose a health hazard to humans. Reseachers have linked this chemical to nervous system disorders and cancer.

Dioxin is only one of many deadly compounds, many of which are waste products of the modern chemical industry. Such *toxic waste* is a problem with over 143 to 440 tons (130 to 400 metric tons) produced annually in this country. These compounds are often very stable and last for years. The solution to date has been disposal, often burial, at one of 20,000 toxic waste dumps.

Such dumps are at best an unsatisfactory solution to this problem. Too often, the toxic chemicals leak out and enter drinking water of nearby communities. Sometimes, the sites are forgotten, and developers put up houses on top of them.

The EPA has banned the manufacture and use of some of these chemicals such as PCP, an electrical insulating fluid, but this does not help dispose of the material already in exis-

Hazardous-waste technicians covering excavated contaminated soil to keep down airborne particles

tence or those toxic chemicals too valuable in industry to ban. Thus, chemists have turned their efforts to finding real ways of disposing of toxic waste.

The major drawback of dumps and landfills is that they leak. Keenan Strinivasan of the University of Michigan has discovered that dioxin as well as other toxic compounds will bond firmly into a mixture of clay and aluminum. Strinivasan feels that filters made from this clay-aluminum mix could be placed so as to purify industrial wastewater. As the water flowed through, the filter would remove the toxic chemicals. Also, since it appears to be "leakproof," the mix could provide a secure lining for dumps and landfills.

Even if Strinivasan and other chemists do present us with safe places to dump future toxic waste, what do we do about that which is already loose in the land and water? There are chemical methods of isolating and dissolving compounds such as dioxin, but it is expensive and difficult to treat chemically tons of soil or water.

According to Daniel Crosby of the University of California, Davis, ultraviolet light—the same solar radiation that tans our skins—may be the best weapon against dioxin. Under sunlight or UV from mercury arc lamps, dioxin breaks down into harmless compounds.

While these searches for containment and destruction of toxic chemicals proceed, two chemists, Paul Jackson and Nigel Robinson of Los Alamos National Laboratory, have been looking for a way to protect crops from being poisoned by such compounds. They recently announced a carbon-based compound that keeps plants from taking up toxic metals such as cadmium and copper and dying.

TOO HOT TO HANDLE

If anything is capable of arousing people's fear more than toxic waste, it is radioactive waste. Such material, particularly spent nuclear fuel often high in plutonium, poses a special problem because it remains radioactively dangerous for hundreds, sometimes thousands of years.

At present, the only plan for nuclear waste is to bury it.

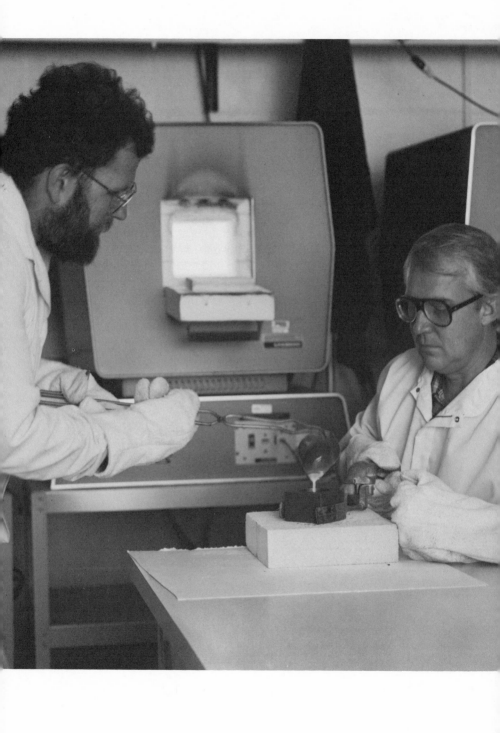

Research is needed to find ways to contain this waste so that it cannot find its way into soil and drinking water.

One solution is to make the waste part of the container holding it. Using either boron or lead glass, scientists heat both the glass and the nuclear waste until liquid. They then mix the two materials together and allow the mixture to cool. The result is a glass jar that chemically traps the waste within, and if this exceptionally strong glass should break, there can be no spillage. Such glass is also resistant to corrosive chemicals that might be in the surrounding ground.

Paul Huray of Oak Ridge has a slightly different way of chemically holding plutonium waste. By mixing plutonium with phosphorus, Huray creates a solid that is chemically stable and insoluble in water, so the waste would again be unable to escape into the environment.

The dangers that both chemical and nuclear wastes pose are real, and there is no doubt that something should have been done about them long ago. But the chemical menace of these compounds has only been fully recognized within the last few decades. Nor should we forget that the problem of toxic waste is not merely a scientific one, but a political and economic problem as well, and this complicates the final solution.

We should also not think that chemistry is the only approach to solving this chemical hazard. Biologists are experimenting with bacteria that seem to thrive on toxic waste, turning it into less harmful compounds. Also, companies such as Polysar Biox and DuPont are finding ways of turning one industry's waste into another's raw materials (compounds thrown away by oil refineries are being turned into plastics, for example). We can only hope that these efforts are neither too little nor too late.

Preparing a sample of special glass containing simulated nuclear waste. Upon cooling, the radioactive elements in the solid waste would become chemically incorporated in the glass structure.

CHAPTER 10
OUR CHEMICAL FUTURE

*I*n the previous chapters, we have seen that chemistry is so varied a field that it would be difficult to find a science or a discipline which is not presently affected by chemical research and development. Whether it be making microscopic beads for instrument calibration or pocket-sized machines or new drugs, chemistry has a role. It also continues revealing more and more to us about the structure of molecules, presenting us with new chemical elements, and providing us with information about humanity's past. The revolutions of chemistry are not just important to the chemist but to our entire world.

And the future?

We can expect the revolutions of the present to carry on into future years. Computers will become more and more important to chemical research, particularly computer simulation. It shouldn't be long before examination of molecular structure of even the most complicated compound will be routine. We can also expect to see many, if not all, chemical processes tested through computer simulation before actual lab runs are made: The savings in time and cost will be considerable.

Genetic engineering, alteration of DNA for specific purposes such as the production of drugs, will be an increasingly important revolution for chemistry and biology. Already this revolution is producing human insulin. In the future, we may see many industrial processes taken over by chemically altered microorganisms. Such biological manufacturing seems to promise fewer pollution risks, although there are still many unanswered questions about genetic engineering for future chemists and biologists to face.

Our future chemical world is being built right now. What chemists are doing today will affect us in the 1990s and beyond. Let us take a quick look at some of the potential future revolutions in chemistry and their possible consequences on our lives.

CLEANING UP THE FUTURE

In the last chapter, we looked at some of the pollution problems created by our chemical world. The search for ways of dealing with these problems is and will continue to be in part a chemical one.

One of the major sources of air pollution in the U.S. is the automobile. We are a country constantly on the move, and our millions of cars not only provide us with the ability to travel but also with large amounts of pollutants such as carbon monoxide and sulfur dioxide.

Since an outright ban on automobiles is not likely, the obvious solution is to replace the internal combustion engine and eliminate the poisonous by-products of burning gasoline. One alternative to the gasoline-powered car is the electric car.

To date, the electric car has been confined mostly to novelty stories on the evening news, in which the inventor opens up a car trunk to reveal tightly packed batteries. And that is the problem with the electric car: batteries. The inconvenience of having to spend several hours every 100 miles (1,600 kilometers) or so recharging those batteries has done nothing to popularize the electric car.

Does chemistry have an answer? Possibly—in the *fuel cell.* Although fuel cells operate like batteries, they do not have to be recharged since a continuous stream of fuel enters them. The most common fuel cells use hydrogen and oxygen, and as these two compounds react to form water, they generate an electric current.

The fuel cell is not new, but until recently, its use was restricted mostly to spacecraft such as Gemini and Apollo in the 1960s, which used dangerous hydrazine. (It was the explosion of a hydrazine fuel cell that crippled *Apollo 13*.) Unfortunately, a hydrogen fuel cell puts out only 1.3 volts, not even as much as the AA batteries that power small calculators.

Since the late 1970s, however, researchers such as Byron McCormick of Los Alamos National Laboratory have been working on developing new commercial fuel cells capable of safely powering an automobile. McCormick is investigating the use of methanol in place of hydrogen. Methanol, which can be obtained by processing garbage, would be an inexpensive fuel, costing about fifty cents a gallon. Although not quite as pollution-free as a hydrogen-oxygen fuel cell, the methanol cell would produce far fewer pollutants than present gasoline-burning car engines.

LIGHTING THE FUTURE

The future fuel cell may provide power for more than just automobiles. In the early 1980s, United Technologies Corporation developed, under a Department of Energy contract, a fuel cell to be used by power plants. The 10-square-foot (1-square-meter) cells are arranged in stacks. Each stack consists of 400 to 500 fuel cells and generates eleven megawatts, enough power to supply electricity to half a million homes.

In New York City, Consolidated Edison is testing a pilot fuel cell plant. This plant puts out almost five megawatts and so far seems quite successful.

In Tempe, Arizona, other kinds of plants—green, growing ones—may be showing the way to efficient, practical solar energy cells. Present-day solar cells are both bulky and often unreliable. Daily, however, billions of plants turn sunlight into energy and food for themselves through a chemical process called *photosynthesis.*

For years, scientists have been attempting to duplicate photosynthesis in the labs, but the process is complicated and not fully understood. Researchers do know that the energy from the Sun kicks loose an electron from one com-

Left: *fuel cell power plant (bottom of photograph) in New York, New York. Note the absence of smokestacks.* Above: *Fuel cells before being shipped to the New York power plant.*

pound, sending it hopping through a whole series of other compounds. While the electron is in this molecular circuit, the original molecule undergoes a reaction that begins the conversion of carbon dioxide and water into oxygen and food.

At Arizona State University, Devens Gust and Thomas A. Moore set up a series of three molecules. They knocked loose an electron from the first molecule, but before it could react, the maverick electron had jumped to the second and third molecules and back to the first.

Still, Gust and Moore's experiment ran 10,000 times longer than past attempts. They realize, however, that three-millionths of a second is not long enough for artificial photosynthesis and feel they must add more compounds, perhaps up to seven, before they will be successful. If this testing is successful, we may someday be powering our homes using the same chemistry that keeps houseplants alive.

INSULATING THE FUTURE

Winter. Outside it is well below freezing, but inside your home you are warm, completely surrounded by walls packed with plenty of efficient insulation. Well, almost surrounded, you realize, as you stand by a window and feel the cold seep in. What you feel, however, is not cold coming inside; it is a temperature drop caused by heat flowing *out* the window. A layer or two of glass is just not capable of insulating as well as the several inches of fiberglass batting in the walls.

Stephen Selkowitz of Lawrence Berkley Laboratory may have a "chemical window" that will do as good a job of insulating as that fiberglass. Selkowitz is working with aerogels—jellylike silicon compounds. He has found that a window made from a slab of aerogel 1 inch (2.5 centimeters) thick insulates as well as 3 inches (7.5 centimeters) of fiberglass.

Unfortunately, you will not find these windows on the market for a few years yet. Besides not being strong enough to make practical windows, aerogels also distort light entering through them. An aerogel window appears green, and objects seen through it look red!

*Aerogel, a new
insulating substance*

COMPUTING THE FUTURE

In the 1966 movie *Fantastic Voyage*, scientists shrink a submarine with its human crew and inject them into a patient's bloodstream. The crew is to travel to the patient's brain and remove an inoperable blood clot.

Because of its premise, this movie is not even science fiction; it is fantasy, since such shrinkage is impossible. What may *not* be impossible in the next few decades are microscopic robots, physically able to enter a patient's body and intelligent enough to deal with tumors, blood clots, and other abnormal masses that conventional surgery cannot reach. Or at least such will be possible if chemist Forrest L. Carter of Naval Research Laboratory and other attendees of the Second International Workshop on Molecular Electronic Devices are right.

These scientists are beginning the long program to develop a computer whose circuitry is not made of integrated circuits but of molecules. Instead of depending on a flow of electrons to function, such molecular computers would operate through the movement of atoms in chemical reactions.

What would be the advantage of molecular computers as compared to the present-day silicon chip models? For one, size. A computer is made up of a great many on-off switches, and it performs its functions by running through different combinations of these switches. However, even with the best integrated circuit, each of these on-off switches requires billions of atoms.

The molecular computer will use one molecule for every on-off switch. Even if the largest protein molecules were needed for such switches, no switch would use more than a million atoms. Each of these molecular switches would be at least a thousand times smaller than the contemporary semiconductor switches. Carter thinks that a molecular computer the size of a sugar cube would have a billion more switches than the best computer available today, and the larger the number of on-off switches, the larger the number of functions a computer can perform.

The molecular computer may have other advantages over our present models—it may be capable of imitating the operation of the human brain. The human brain *is* a molecular computer, all of its work done through the movement of atoms in chemical reactions. A computer that worked like our brains would be capable of doing several things at once. At the same time you read this page, you can also eat a sandwich, shift around in your chair, listen to music. And these represent only a conscious use of your brain. Your brain is also keeping your heart beating and your lungs pumping, watching for invading viruses, manufacturing blood cells in the spleen and bone marrow, and so forth.

Our modern computers cannot do such parallel operations. They do one thing at a time, but they do it so fast—in billionths of a second—they seem to be doing many different jobs at once. Imagine the speed of a computer that could actually perform parallel operations.

The work on molecular computers is just beginning, and when such computers may be available to us is difficult to say. Chemists still need to develop the chemical switches. One promising candidate is a class of compounds that alter their molecular structure when exposed to light. When the light disappears, the compounds revert to their original structure, and then the process can be repeated. Light pulses could, therefore, turn these on and off.

So somewhere in our chemical future, we may have molecular computers running medical implants that give sight to the blind and hearing to the deaf, operating body monitors on the lookout for disease, or feeding data directly into the brain of an airline pilot. For better or worse, they may be the real thing: *thinking* machines.

The future revolutions of chemistry are starting today. We can be sure that these revolutions will affect us as the past and present revolutions already are doing. As chemists learn more about chemical properties and discover new compounds, they will lead us to a world with more and more chemistry in our daily lives.

GLOSSARY

Alpha Particles. A form of radiation given off by radioactive material.

Atom. The smallest particle of matter capable of taking part in a chemical reaction. It has three primary subparticles, the electron, the proton, and the neutron.

Atomic Nucleus. The core of an atom, in which are grouped all of the protons and neutrons. The plural is *nuclei.*

Atomic Number. The number of protons an atom possesses; it also identifies the element of the atom.

Beta Particles. A form of radiation given off by radioactive material.

Biochemists. Those who study the chemistry of living things.

Ceramics. Materials made from baking clay composed of silicon and aluminium oxides.

Chain Reaction. The multiple release of neutrons by every atom split in a nuclear fission reaction, so that the number of atoms fissioning doubles and triples each second the reaction lasts.

Chemical Bond. The linkage that holds atoms together in a molecule and that is formed by the sharing of electrons.

Chemical Compound. Any substance composed of molecules of the same atomic structure and composition.

Chemical Element. Any substance all of whose atoms have the same atomic number. Of the 100+ known elements, uranium (atomic number 92) is the largest one that occurs naturally.

Chemical Reaction. The process by which molecules of two or more compounds exchange atoms to form new and different compounds.

Chemistry. The study of materials to understand their compositions, properties, and interactions. Such understanding is based on atomic theory.

Chlorofluorocarbons. Compounds used as coolants in refrigerators and air conditioners and linked to the destruction of ozone in the upper atmosphere.

Composites. Any substance composed of two parts, a resin (a polymer) and whiskers (reinforcing fibers). The resin keeps the whiskers from breaking, and the whiskers strengthen the resin; thus together, the two are stronger than either individually.

Critical Mass. The amount of fissionable material needed for a self-sustaining chain reaction.

Dioxin. An extremely toxic compound that forms part of some herbicides, plant killers.

DNA. The chemical compound in plants and animals that passes on inherited characteristics from parent to offspring.

Electron. One of the three primary subatomic particles, having a negative charge and orbiting around the atomic nucleus. It is also the part of the atom that forms chemical bonds.

Food Additives. Chemical compounds added to food to increase its nutritional value or to preserve it.

Fuel Cell. Using a continuous flow of fuel to produce a chemical reaction, it generates electrical power.

Gamma Rays. A form of radiation given off by radioactive material.

Gas Chromatography Column. A device that separates chemical compounds according to size.

Geochemists. Researchers who study the chemistry of the Earth.

Half-life. A property of radioactive elements in which half of any given amount of such material will disappear through radioactive decay after a specific length of time.

Heart Pacemaker. A device implanted into the chest of a patient suffering from an irregularly beating heart. The implant electronically stimulates the heart muscles to keep the heart beating steadily.

Integrated Circuits. An electronic component in which the circuit and transistors are all one unit.

Isotope. Atoms that have the same atomic number (are the same element) but have different numbers of neutrons. These isotopes can be radioactive and used in radioactive tracers.

Mass Spectrometer. An instrument that determines molecular structure by breaking molecules into fragments.

Molecule. Any combination of atoms linked by chemical bonds.

Neutron. One of the three primary subatomic particles, having no charge and located in the atomic nucleus.

Nuclear Fission. The splitting of the nucleus of a large atom, normally with a neutron, into the nuclei of atoms having smaller atomic numbers.

Nuclear Fusion. The forceful merging of the nuclei of two smaller atoms to form one of greater atomic number.

Nuclear Reaction. The spontaneous change, accompanied by released radiation, of the atoms of one element into those of another element.

Nuclear Reactor. A sealed vessel at the heart of a nuclear power plant in which the nuclear fission process occurs.

Oxide. A chemical compound in which one or more elements bond with oxygen.

Ozone. A molecule composed of three oxygen atoms.

Pesticide. Any chemical compound designed to kill insect pests.

Pharmaceutical Industry. The industry that manages both prescription and nonprescription drugs.

Photosynthesis. The chemical process by which green plants use sunlight to convert carbon dioxide and water into oxygen and food.

Plastic. Any polymer, although generally carbon-based, that can be molded using heat or pressure.

Polymer. Any long-chained molecule, although the most common have a carbon spine.

Proteins. Very large carbon-containing molecules that are the building blocks of living matter.

Proton. One of the three primary subatomic particles, having a positive charge and located in the atomic nucleus. The number of protons an atom has is its atomic number.

Radiation. Energy released from radioactively decaying material. Radiation takes three forms: alpha particles, beta particles, and gamma rays.

Radioactive. Any element whose atoms are undergoing a nuclear reaction and is accompanied by a release of radiation.

Radioactive Decay. A nuclear reaction.

Radioactive Tracer. Any compound possessing a radioactive isotope, used in following chemical reactions, checking on liquid flow patterns, making medical diagnoses, etc.

Semiconductor. Materials that at room temperature carry electricity better than insulators, but not as well as conductors. Their conductivity can be increased with chemical additives.

Silicones. Polymers consisting of alternating silicon and oxygen atoms.

Superconductors. A material that has no resistance to electricity.

Tandem Mass Spectrometer. Two mass spectrometers linked together, so that unknown chemicals can be both separated from one another and then structurally analyzed.

Toxic Waste. Dangerous chemicals left after the completion of many industrial processes.

Trace Elements. Any chemical element such as iron or copper needed in small amounts by humans to maintain good health.

Transistor. Composed of two semiconductors, it controls or amplifies electrical current in electronic circuitry.

Transmutation. To change one chemical element into another through a nuclear reaction.

Transuranics. Any chemical element having an atomic number higher than uranium's 92; none of these occur in nature.

Virus. A microorganism often responsible for disease.

Vitamins. Nitrogen-containing compounds that regulate the body's use of chemicals that come from food.

X-ray Spectrometer. An instrument that maps out molecular structure using X-rays.

SELECTED READING

Asimov, Isaac. *Asimov on Chemistry.* New York: Doubleday, 1974.

Brady, James E., and Gerard E. Huniston. *General Chemistry: Principles and Structure.* New York: Wiley, 1982.

Chemistry Education Association. *Chemistry: Key to the Earth.* 1979.

Companion, Audrey L. *Chemical Bonding.* New York: McGraw-Hill, 1979.

Creighton, Thomas E. *Proteins: Structures and Molecular Properties.* New York: Freeman, 1984.

Cremlyn, R. *Pesticides: Preparation and Modes of Action.* New York: Wiley, 1978.

Daintith, John, ed. *Dictionary of Chemistry.* New York: Harper & Row, 1982.

Epstein, Samuel et al. *Hazardous Waste in America.* San Francisco: Sierra Club, 1980.

Gardner, Robert. *Kitchen Chemistry.* New York: Simon & Schuster, 1983.

Hill, John W. *Chemistry for Changing Times.* Minneapolis: Burgess, 1980.

McQuarrie, Donald A., and Peter A. Rock. *Descriptive Chemistry.* New York: Freeman, 1985.

Neubauer, Alfred. *Chemistry Today: A Portrait of a Science.* New York: Arco, 1983.

Parker, Sybil P., ed. *McGraw-Hill Dictionary of Chemistry.* New York: McGraw-Hill, 1984.

Ross, Frank, Jr. *The Magic Chip: Exploring Microelectronics.* New York: Simon & Schuster, 1984.

Selinger, Ben. *Chemistry in the Market Place*. Canberra: Australian National University Press, 1978.

Sherwood, Martin. *The New Chemistry*. New York: Basic, 1974.

Steele, Gerald L. *Exploring the World of Plastics*. New York: Taplinger, 1977.

Stine, William R. *Chemistry for the Consumer*. Newton, Mass.: Allyn & Bacon, 1978.

Tocci, Salvatore. *Chemistry with Everyday Products*. New York: Arco, 1985.

For recent information on chemistry, consult the following magazines:

Discover
Science '86
Science Digest
Science News
Scientific American

INDEX

Kevlar, 35, 37
Kopple, Kenneth, 39
Krypton, 56
Kwalek, Stephanie, 37

Langmuir, Irving, 18
Levinthal, Cyrus, 25
Lewis, Gilbert, 18
Libby, Willard, 77
Lupinski, John, 39

MacDiarmid, Alan, 39
Mass spectrometer, 19, 121
Matthews, Dennis, 23
McCormick, Byron, 111
McGee, Kenneth, 73
Medical diagnosis, 60
Molecules, 15, 24, 25, 27, 121

Neutron, 16, 121
Nuclear fission, 56, 122
Nuclear fuels, 68
Nuclear fusion, 63–64, 122
Nuclear power plant, 57, 59
Nuclear reaction, 55–56, 60, 122
Nuclear reactor, 59
Nylon, 37

Oxides, 47, 122
Ozone, 102–103, 122

Pauling, Linus, 19, 20
Pesticides, 97, 99, 100, 122
Plastic, 27, 28–29, 31, 34–35, 122
Plutonium, 65, 66
PNP, 93
Pollution, 101–102, 110–111
Polycarbonate, 32
Polyethylene, 30, 32, 37
Polyform, 34–35
Polymers, 28, 37, 38, 45, 82, 122
Polystyrene, 31, 34
Proteins, 21, 122

Proton, 16, 122

Radiation, 55, 63, 123
Radioactive decay, 55, 57, 123
Radioactive isotopes, 59, 60, 77
Radioactive tracer, 59, 123
Radioactive waste, 105, 107
Radioactivity, 56, 123
Rochow, Eugene, 83
Rugg, Charles, 93
Rutherford, Lord, 16

Seaborg, Glen, 66
Selkowitz, Stephen, 114
Semiconductors, 85, 123
Shockley, William, 86
Silicon, 81–83, 123
Silicon chips, 84, 85, 86, 88, 89
Spectrometer system, 22
Strassmann, Fritz, 56
Superconductor, 88, 123
Synthetic fibers, 37

Tandem mass spectrometer, 21, 123
Toxic waste, 103, 105, 123
Trace elements, 96, 123
Tracers, 59, 60
Transistor, 40, 86, 123
Transmutation, 64, 123
Transuranics, 65–66, 124

Uranium-235, 68

Virus, 92, 124
Vitamins, 94–95, 124

Walker, Charles, 94, 95
Warburg, Otto, 94
Watson, James, 13
Wheeler, W., 50
Wrighton, Mark S., 39

X-ray laser, 23
X-ray spectrometer, 23, 124